EVERYDAY COOKING WITH JACQUES PÉPIN

Also by Jacques Pépin

La Méthode

La Technique

A French Chef Cooks at Home

EVERYDAY COOKING WITH JACQUES PÉPIN

HARPER & ROW, PUBLISHERS, NEW YORK

CAMBRIDGE • PHILADELPHIA • SAN FRANCISCO • LONDON

MEXICO CITY • SÃO PAULO • SYDNEY

Jacques Pépin's new television series is a
presentation of WJCT-TV in Jacksonville, Florida.
Broadcasting on PBS stations is made possible
by a grant from Cuisinarts, Inc.

Portions of this book previously
appeared in *The Ladies' Home Journal*.

E V E R Y D A Y   C O O K I N G   W I T H   J A C Q U E S   P É P I N
Copyright © 1982 by Jacques Pépin

Photographs by Leon Perer
Additional photographs by Tom Hopkins

Library of Congress Cataloging in Publication Data
Pépin, Jacques.
Everyday cooking with Jacques Pépin.
Includes index.
1. Cookery, French. I. Title.
TX719.P458   641.5944   81-48047
AACR2
ISBN 0-06-014994-9   82 83 84 85 86 10 9 8 7 6 5 4 3 2 1
ISBN 0-06-090943-9 (pbk.)   82 83 84 85 86 10 9 8 7 6 5 4 3 2 1

To the home cook, the source of all good food

C O N T E N T S

T H E   R E C I P E S

S O U P S   A N D   B R E A D S

E G G   D I S H E S

S H E L L F I S H   A N D   F I S H

P O U L T R Y

M E A T S

P A S T A ,   R I C E ,   A N D   P O T A T O E S

When we sat down to plan the television series that gave its name to this book, it was clear from the start that both the book and the television series—at this point I almost can't remember which came first—were to be about saving money and, where possible, time in the kitchen. This was to be the underlying theme, but more importantly I wanted to celebrate unpretentious, simple well-cooked food. I wanted to talk about *everyday* cooking, about food that is satisfying, relatively quick to prepare, and also economical—the old-fashioned family food my mother and grandmother raised my brothers and me on. Casting a last glance at the recipes in this book before it goes off to the printer, and with the filming of the show behind us, I feel we really accomplished what we set out to do, holding true to those early intentions.

In a funny way, I can't truly say that I created anything special for this book. Somehow these recipes were always there, either in my head or in my heart or in my memory. Some are extrapolated from what we eat day to day in our home; and others, like the Sausage and Potato Stew (page 109) or the Potato Ragoût (page 121), are plucked whole from my memory of the food I ate growing up in Bourg-en-Bresse and Lyon. The Eggs Jeannette I've named after my mother, who served them to us often when my brothers and I were small. Still others are completely the result of invention and circumstance, determined by what's in the refrigerator, who stops by, what's in the garden—a "cuisine d'opportunité." Finally, lots of these recipes are just the results of plain, old-fashioned common sense, like binding leftover pasta shells with cheese and eggs for a gratin (page 41), or turning pieces of leftover roast into meatballs (Boulettes of Beef, page 125), or a mashed potato–topped stew (Gratin Parmentier, page 123). In retrospect, I realize these recipes are perhaps more a part of me than the recipes in any of my other books, because these dishes are not those acquired during the many years I apprenticed and worked in restaurants, but are recipes that are really innate.

My intention in this book is to encourage you to look at the ingredients in your refrigerator in a new light, to pay more respect to certain staples that are always in the house, and to realize that there are wonderful meals that can be made out of almost anything you have at home—truly, one doesn't have to spend much money or time to make a gratifying and delectable meal.

To turn leftovers into stews or gratins, or bits of meat into salads, to transform vegetables into fritters or bones into soup—these are very simple concepts that should become second nature. It is my hope that they will become part of your day-to-day repertoire, used week after week, year after year, becoming so associated with your own cuisine that another generation will be naming these dishes after you.

LEFTOVERS: It makes me feel uncomfortable when people are apologetic about serving leftovers, because if the cook is good there should be no reason to apologize. You will find there are lots of recipes that make use of leftovers in this book. Born to a family of restaurateurs and having worked all my life in the world of food, I find it's second nature to be thrifty and avoid spoilage. I actually hurt when I see food rotting in the refrigerator or people throwing out things like bones which could be used for a flavorful base for dishes like the Fish Soup (page 24) or the Chicken Cassoulet (page 98).

In the normal working of a professional kitchen, the chefs save food instinctively. The meat is trimmed, the trimmings are turned into ground meat and the bones go into a stock which may be turned into a sauce, and so on. Things move naturally in a logical progression, everything is used in an endless cycle, and practically nothing is discarded. By the same token, at home a good cook should be able to transform a dish and extend its use by making it into a fresh and different creation, rather than a second-rate version of the original.

The most common mistake made with leftovers is to try to preserve the food in its original form. Roast beef will never be a hot roast beef again because it doesn't reheat well. However, cold roast beef served with condiments and a salad is excellent, while sliced and sautéed with onions, garlic and beef broth, it makes a wonderful Beef Mironton (page 123). Similarly, a perfectly roasted chicken will never taste as good reheated, but turned into a cold salad it tastes fresh again. On the other hand, stews, as well as most soups, often taste better after reheating, and pâté is usually more flavorful the third or fourth day.

SAVING TIME IN THE KITCHEN: When it comes to saving time in the kitchen, there are certain deceptively simple things to keep in mind. For example, you'll never see a professional chef start to make a simple mushroom omelet by breaking the eggs and then slicing the mushrooms. He'll first put a pat of butter in a skillet, set it on the heat, and by the time the skillet is ready, the one or two mushrooms will have been sliced and the one or two eggs broken. No time is lost sitting around waiting for the butter to melt. In your own kitchen, try to think things through for yourself. Always start with the task that takes the longest, though it might seem a trivial part of the recipe. Save clean-up time by laying out newspapers when you peel and clean vegetables so you can toss out the peels and newspapers all at once. If you plan to make soup, cook pasta, or boil vegetables for dinner, put a pot of water on the stove to boil first, even before assembling ingredients.

Beware of opaque plastic containers or wrapping things in foil. These foods can easily get lost in the refrigerator and slowly rot unseen. Look and think before you start cooking: Can I use this? Or that? A piece of carrot, onion, or celery can go in some soup or in a stew. Even if a recipe has to be twisted and changed, use the food and don't let it rot. Recipes aren't static, especially in simple everyday cooking. Ingredients rarely have to follow the recipe exactly. If you understand a dish, then you will know what you can add or subtract and how to change it. This comes easily with a little knowledge and experience, and the best way to acquire both is to get behind the stove and cook.

Happy times! Happy cooking!

U indicates preparation time

C indicates cooking time

U C indicates combined preparation and cooking time

We were a bit overenthusiastic when we planned our programs; we had hoped to demonstrate one whole menu per show. Of course, each half hour turned out to be barely enough to cover all the things I had to say about just one dish, let alone a three-course menu. Those of you who are following the television series will recognize the starred dishes as the ones demonstrated. The accompanying courses were just shown briefly. But in the pages that follow, for viewers and nonviewers alike we finally cover it all. These menus, which are highly personal and subjective, probably tell more about my tastes and habits as a cook than anything else. Remember that they are arbitrary and the different dishes can be reassembled into infinite combinations to reflect your own tastes more accurately.

Lettuce soufflé
Sautéed whiting Grenoble style
Herbed zucchini
Apple fritters

Chicken liver pâté*
Gratin of pasta
Pears in red wine

Fish soup*
Fried eggplant
Jam omelet

Gratin of cabbage
Stew of chicken wings*
Croûte of fruit

Celery soup
Sausage and potato stew
Escarole salad
Apple galette*

Marinated peppers
Pilaff of mussels*
Flambéed bananas

Vegetable soup*
Mackerel in vinaigrette
Peach gratiné

Oatmeal panbread
Chicken cassoulet*
Boston lettuce and cracklings
Crystallized grapes and oranges

Carrot and walnut salad
Cucumber salad

Eggs Jeannette* or
Gratin of eggs*

Citrus and raisin compote

Parisienne gnocchi*
Boulettes of beef
Cabbage salad
Melon in honey

Corn chowder
Chicken livers sautéed with vinegar
Stewed crinkled kale
Crêpes with jam*

Tomato salad
Potato ragoût
Poached oranges with candied rinds*

Potato lace
Stuffed breast of lamb*
Apple bonne femme

Bread galette
Gratin parmentier*
Mocha and chocolate cream

Onions and carrots Greek style
Mayonnaise of chicken*
or
Mayonnaise of fish*
Cream puff fritters

---

* Asterisked dishes are demonstrated on the television series Everyday Cooking with Jacques Pépin.

FIRST COURSES & ACCOMPANIMENTS

SOUPS AND BREADS

Vegetable Soup / Baked Corn Dumplings

Fish Soup / Garlic Croûtons

Celery Soup / Cold Cream of Celery Soup

Corn Chowder / Oyster Corn Chowder

Oatmeal Panbread

Bread Galette / Fruit Bread Pancake

EGGS AND SUCH

Eggs Jeannette   Gratin of Eggs   Parisienne Gnocchi

Gratin of Pasta and Vegetables / Pasta Cake

Lettuce Soufflé / Gratin Soufflé / Cold Soufflé Vinaigrette

PÂTÉ

Chicken Liver Pâté / Melba Toast

VEGETABLES

Fried Eggplant

Gratin of Cabbage

Stewed Crinkled Kale

Herbed Zucchini

Potato Lace

SALADS

Cabbage Salad

Onions and Carrots Greek Style

Marinated Peppers

Carrot and Walnut Salad

Cucumber Salad

Tomato Salad with Onion

Tomato Salad with Basil

This sturdy vegetable soup, almost a stew, is a particularly good one-dish meal in summer and early fall when fresh vegetables are plentiful. Almost any vegetable can be used, but it is best to balance strong vegetables, such as yellow turnips or cabbage, with vegetables that have a less pronounced flavor, such as potatoes or carrots. Do not feel limited by our list of ingredients. Use whatever the market has to offer, or make do with leftovers from the refrigerator—some wilted lettuce, scallions, pieces of celery, or carrots. The stronger and tighter the vegetable—green pepper, butternut squash, and carrots, for example—the smaller the pieces should be (about 1/2-inch dice). Softer vegetables, such as eggplant and zucchini, should be cut into 1-inch dice. Lettuce or spinach leaves can be left whole or cut into halves.

The mixture added to the soup at the end is what gives it its distinctive taste. The mixture of basil, garlic, cheese, and olive oil is called *pistou*, and by extension the soup itself is often called *pistou* or *soupe au pistou.* It is a specialty of the south of France. Note its similarity to *pesto.* In the summer, when you have access to fresh basil, you should prepare large batches in a food processor, divide it into 1/2- or 1-cup containers, and freeze. Add the frozen block to the soup 10 to 15 minutes before serving, bring to a boil, and let it melt. The *pistou* can be omitted for people who are not fond of garlic and you'll still have a very good vegetable soup.

4 ounces salt pork or bacon or 1/3 cup vegetable oil

1 1/2 cups diced onions

1 1/2 cups diced celery (the leafy part is the most flavorful)

2 cups loosely packed sliced scallions and leeks, mixed

1 medium-sized green pepper, seeded and diced (2/3 cup)

9 cups water

1 tablespoon salt

1 1/2 cups diced carrots

1 1/2 cups unpeeled and diced eggplant

1 1/2 cups peeled and diced butternut squash

1 cup peeled and diced kohlrabi

1 1/2 cups peeled and diced potatoes

1 1/2 cups diced zucchini

1 cup cut-up string beans

1 cup lettuce leaves

2 cups spinach leaves

SERVES 8 TO 10

⏱ 25 TO 30 MINUTES

🍲 50 TO 60 MINUTES

The corn dumplings are optional, but they add texture to the soup and make it heartier. They are not poached in the soup, which is the conventional method, but baked in the oven so that they become golden and crusty on top. When they are added to the soup they absorb some of the liquid and get a bit soft, but still hold their shape quite well. The dumplings could be replaced with pasta, such as noodles or elbow macaroni, added 15 to 20 minutes before the end of the cooking.

This soup can be made ahead, reheated, and even frozen.

1 Cut the salt pork or bacon into ½-inch pieces. Fry them in a large pot until they sizzle. Cook for 5 to 6 minutes over medium heat until the pieces are nicely crisp and brown. Add the onions, celery, scallions, and green pepper and sauté for 2 to 3 minutes.

2 Add the water, salt, and remaining vegetables except the lettuce and spinach. Bring to a boil. Lower the heat, cover, and simmer for 45 minutes.

Add the lettuce and spinach, and cook for another 15 minutes. During that time prepare the *pistou* and dumplings.

PISTOU

The *pistou* can be used to enhance other types of soups in addition to this one and is also very good tossed with steamed vegetables, sautéed potatoes or cooked pasta.

1 cup basil leaves or parsley leaves, or a mixture of both

1 Purée all the ingredients in the bowl of a food processor until smooth.

4 cloves garlic, peeled

¼ cup Parmesan cheese

2 Stir the *pistou* into the soup and bring to a boil. Serve with corn dumplings.

¼ cup olive oil or vegetable oil

BAKED CORN DUMPLINGS

These dumplings are basically a corn bread and can be served with any meal, not just soup.

½ cup cornmeal

1 cup flour

2 teaspoons double-acting baking powder

1 In a bowl combine all the ingredients except the oil and mix well.

1 teaspoon salt

2 eggs

2 Oil one or two large cookie sheets and place large tablespoons of the mixture on top. You should have approximately 16 dumplings. Sprinkle the top with the remaining oil, and bake in a 375-degree oven for 13 to 15 minutes.

½ cup milk

4 tablespoons oil

3 Place the dumplings in the soup 1 or 2 minutes before serving so that they absorb some of the liquid and get soft. Or pass them separately.

Fish is quite expensive nowadays, but you can make great soups and chowders with the parts of the fish that are free. Actually it's these parts—the bones and the heads—that give fish stocks, soups, and stews their taste. The best bones are from flat fish, such as sole, dab, flounder, or halibut, though you can use most any fish as long as it's not oily. (Here we use porgy.) Oily fish, such as mackerel, bluefish, salmon, herring, and tuna, do not have as good a taste; also, the skin is fatty and should be discarded. Collarbones from cod are very good as they yield a great deal of flesh.

When free bones and heads are in the offing, I'll always take advantage of them. When they're not, I'll buy whole fish and have the fishmonger gut and fillet them, reserving the heads and bones for soup, and the fillets for a dish like Fish Fillets Niçoise on page 82. Alternatively, if I buy a whole fish and fillet it for dinner, I'll freeze the heads and bones for later use.

The bones and heads are sautéed quickly, then cooked in water. If there's flesh on the bones, I pick it off after they have been cooked. However, there's not always enough to bother with. Either way the bones and heads are discarded after they have been cooked and picked clean.

Fresh fish is always the best, but you can still get good results with frozen fish bones, provided the fish was very fresh, clean, and properly packed when frozen. When using fresh bones, wash them, and remove the gills and any bloody

---

3 pounds of fish bones and heads or, as in our case, the bones and heads of 4 porgies (1 pound each, gutted), plus 1 extra pound of bones

2 tablespoons oil, preferably olive oil

10 cups water

1 cup sliced onions

1 cup diced celery

1 cup diced scallions

½ cup loose parsley leaves

2½ cups diced fresh tomatoes

½ teaspoon anise seed

1 teaspoon turmeric

½ teaspoon tarragon

½ teaspoon rosemary

½ teaspoon thyme leaves

½ teaspoon freshly ground black pepper

2½ teaspoons salt

S E R V E S   8

🜍 🜍 1¼ T O 1½ H O U R S

parts inside or they will be bitter. If frozen, defrost slowly in the refrigerator, then wash well under cold water.

Our fish soup is enriched with a *rouille,* which is a type of mayonnaise. *Rouille* means "rust," which is the color it imparts when added to the soup. The *rouille* can be mixed into the soup or served on the side. Serve with thin, garlic-flavored croûtons made from French baguettes. Both the *rouille* and the croûtons are optional, though they do add flavor to the soup.

1 Wash the bones and heads under cold water. (If you are using whole fish—like the porgy here—bone and fillet them, leaving the skin on. Be sure to remove the gills and wash well. Refrigerate or freeze the fillets for later use.)

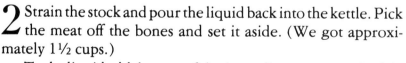

Heat the oil in a large kettle and add the bones and heads. Sauté them in the oil over high heat, stirring, for about 2 minutes. They will break into pieces. Add the water. Bring to a boil, and boil for 15 minutes. If any scum comes to the top, skim it off and discard it.

2 Strain the stock and pour the liquid back into the kettle. Pick the meat off the bones and set it aside. (We got approximately 1½ cups.)

To the liquid add the rest of the ingredients, except the fish, bring to a boil, cover, and boil gently for 35 to 40 minutes.

Strain the stock and purée the solids in a food processor. Return the purée to the liquid and stir to combine. You should have about 8 cups of soup. If you have more, reduce it. If you don't have enough, add water to bring it to 8 cups. Add the pieces of fish and bring the whole mixture back to a boil. Just before serving add the *rouille.*

ROUILLE

1 Process the first four ingredients in a food processor. Add the oil slowly to make a light mayonnaise.

2 Mix some of the *rouille* into the soup, and pass some on the side. Serve the soup in large bowls with croûtons (recipe follows) in it or on the side.

4 to 5 cloves garlic, peeled

¼ cup fish soup

1 whole egg

⅛ teaspoon cayenne pepper

½ cup olive oil or vegetable oil

GARLIC CROÛTONS

1 Spread the vegetable oil on a 16 x 12-inch cookie sheet. Dip the slices of bread in the oil and turn them over. They will pick up a bit of oil on both sides. (This technique is easier than brushing each one with oil.)

2 Place the cookie sheet in a 375-degree oven for 8 to 10 minutes or until the bread is brown and crisp. (Bread browns more uniformly in the oven than under the broiler.)

3 When the bread is cool, rub it lightly with the garlic on both sides. The hard bread abrades like sandpaper and absorbs some of the garlic. Do not use too much—2 cloves should be enough. Serve with soup or salad.

¼ cup vegetable oil

30 slices of stale thin French baguettes, cut no more than ¼ inch thick

2 large cloves garlic, peeled

Stocks are good in soup, but they are not absolutely necessary. Vegetable soups in particular are very good made with water. The soup develops the distinctive taste of the vegetables without any conflicting flavor from the stock.

This Celery Soup, which is made with water, is tasty and inexpensive. If you use large ribs of celery, peel them first, because they are often fibrous. To check, scratch the top of the ribs with your thumbnail to see if there are a lot of strings. Use the leafy parts of the celery, too; they add flavor to the soup.

Many other soups can be prepared in the same manner. You could use a few pieces of left-over vegetables, such as a rib of celery, a bit of lettuce, an onion, or a limp carrot. We purée this soup to make it creamy, but you could grate the vegetables with a hand grater for a different texture. When the vegetables are cut thin, the soup takes only 10 to 15 minutes to cook.

The soup can be thickened in many different ways. Try a piece of bread in each soup bowl or several pieces in a large soup tureen and pour the soup on top. Or thicken it with a *roux* (a mixture of butter and flour), or with potato flour, rice flour, or any kind of pastina or thin noodles. Tapioca, semolina, oatmeal, farina, couscous, and cornmeal are sometimes used to thicken soups. All these thickening agents have one thing in common: they cook within a few minutes and can be added at the last moment.

---

3 cups sliced celery, including some leaves

1 tablespoon butter

1 cup sliced onions

½ cup sliced scallions (including green)

6 cups water

1 teaspoon salt

⅛ teaspoon freshly ground black pepper

½ teaspoon thyme leaves

1½ cups (approximately 2¼ ounces) loose, very thin egg noodles, sometimes called vermicelli

1 cup milk

S E R V E S   6   T O   8

⏱ 10 TO 15 MINUTES

⏱ 30 MINUTES

1 Peel the celery if necessary with a vegetable peeler. (Save the peelings; they can be used in stock.)

2 Melt the butter in a pot, and add the celery, onions, and scallions. Sauté gently over medium heat for about 2 minutes, just enough to soften the vegetables slightly. Add the water, salt, pepper, and thyme. Bring to a boil, cover, and simmer for 15 minutes.

3 Drain the soup and reserve the liquid. Place the solids with a little liquid in a food processor and liquefy; the consistency should be thin.

4 Return the solids and liquid to the pot and add the noodles. Bring to a boil and simmer 3 to 4 minutes, until the noodles are cooked.

5 Add the cup of milk, stir, and serve in individual soup bowls. To make the soup a bit richer, put a dab of fresh butter in each bowl and pour the soup on top. The yield should be approximately 7 cups.

COLD CREAM OF CELERY SOUP

Leftover Celery Soup can be served as a cold soup for the next day. This recipe serves 3 to 4.

3 to 4 cups leftover Celery Soup

½ cup heavy cream

1 tablespoon minced fresh chives or parsley

1 Place the leftover soup in a food processor and purée until smooth. Combine with the heavy cream. Garnish with the minced chives or parsley and serve.
  [Celery Soup on the left; cold Cream of Celery Soup, right.]

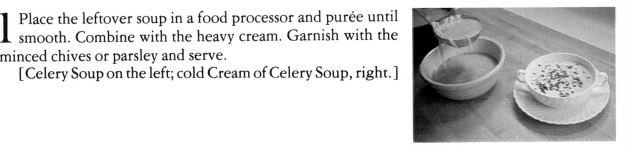

This simple, good soup, made in minutes, is a variation of one my mother and aunts used to make when I was a child, called *soupe au lait,* "milk soup." They used diced scallions or onions, parsley, and a bit of garlic sautéed in butter, to which they added milk, salt, and pepper. After simmering, they poured this infusion into a soup tureen over toasted slices of bread and grated Swiss cheese.

We are great corn aficionados in our family and are always looking for new ways to take advantage of beautiful late summer corn, which is how we came up with this corn chowder variation of the *soupe au lait.* The corn cooks in just a few minutes, which makes it a perfect addition to this very quick soup; the taste also blends well with milk and the other seasonings.

---

3 cups fresh corn kernels (approximately 5 ears of corn)

½ cup grated onion

2 tablespoons butter

½ cup sliced scallions (including green)

4 cups milk

1 teaspoon salt

½ teaspoon freshly ground black pepper

Toasts for garnish (see page 30)

S E R V E S   6

⏱ 10 TO 15 MINUTES

🍳 10 MINUTES

---

1 Husk the corn. Lay each ear flat on the table and separate the kernels from the cob with a long knife. (The more conventional way to remove kernels from the corn is to stand the ear up on end and slice down. However, another safe and easy way of going about the task is to lay the corn cob on its side and slice off the kernels in strips. Use whatever way you find most comfortable.) Grate the onion on the large holes of a hand grater.

Melt the butter in a pot and add the onions and scallions. Sauté over medium heat for about 2 minutes, until the vegetables are soft and sizzling. Add the milk, salt, and pepper, and bring to a boil. When the soup reaches the boiling point, add the corn and stir.

2 As soon as the mixture boils again, remove it from the heat, cover, and let it steep for 2 to 3 minutes. Serve with or without the toasts (recipe follows) on the side, or in the soup if you prefer.

VARIATION—OYSTER CORN CHOWDER: Corn Chowder is exquisite combined with freshly shucked oysters. (Prepare the Corn Chowder through Step 2, then add a dozen and a half shucked oysters with their juice.) The oysters and corn are added at the end so they don't overcook. Sprinkle with fresh herbs and serve—a truly delicate and elegant soup.

TOASTS

1 Cut a thin French baguette into ¼-inch slices. Arrange the bread slices flat on a cookie sheet so they do not overlap.

2 Bake in a 400-degree oven for 8 to 10 minutes, until browned on both sides. They brown without turning.

This versatile quick bread can be served at breakfast, brunch, lunch, or dinner. It is an ideal accompaniment to dishes that are light and in need of substance. It is good served with different types of crudités as a first course, and it is excellent served with cheese. A mixture of chives, basil, tarragon, and other fresh herbs can be used in place of the parsley.

It is at its best when lukewarm. If you make it ahead, reheat it for a few minutes in the oven before serving.

1 cup "quick" oatmeal
2 teaspoons double-acting baking powder
1 cup grated onions
½ cup chopped parsley
1 egg
½ teaspoon salt
¼ teaspoon freshly ground black pepper
½ cup milk
3 tablespoons vegetable oil

S E R V E S   6

⏲ 1 0   M I N U T E S

⏲ 2 5   T O   3 0   M I N U T E S

1 Mix together all the ingredients except the oil. Heat 2 tablespoons of the oil in a 7- to 8-inch skillet. When hot, pour the batter into the skillet and spread the last tablespoon of oil on top of the batter. Bake in a 400-degree oven for 20 minutes. (Wrap two layers of aluminum foil around the handle if it's not oven-proof.)

2 After 20 minutes, flip the bread over to brown the other side. It can be flipped like a crêpe, or inverted on a plate or cake pan and slid back into the skillet. Bake for another 5 to 8 minutes. Slide onto a plate, let cool for 2 or 3 minutes, slice into wedges and serve.

These bread pancakes, which can be made from leftover stale bread, are easy, economical, and take almost no time to prepare. They can replace bread in a meal, or dumplings in a soup. They can be spread with butter for breakfast or brunch. Cheese makes a delicious flavor variation, and fruit transforms them into a dessert or breakfast pancake (recipe follows this one).

Bread sometimes gets moldy, but it is still usable if only partially spoiled. Just cut the moldy part off and the bread will be fine. In recipes like this where bread is mixed with a liquid, the quantity of liquid used should correspond to the dryness of the bread. This is something you have to do by feel.

Bread, especially French-style bread, loses its crispness overnight. Kept in a closed plastic bag, it will keep a bit longer, but it will still get soft. To freshen it, wet lightly by passing it under running water, and place it in a 400-degree oven for 10 to 12 minutes. The bread will become crunchy and crispy again. Serve it right away, because it will dry out fairly fast, get hard, and crumble. (Leftover pieces of bread, whether soft or hard, can be used in this recipe.)

8 ounces leftover bread (one type or a mixture of different breads)

1 cup milk (more or less depending on the dryness of the bread)

4 eggs, lightly beaten as for an omelet

1 cup minced green scallions

½ teaspoon freshly ground black pepper

½ teaspoon salt

Approximately ⅓ cup oil to cook the pancakes

YIELD: 12 PANCAKES
TO SERVE 6

🕐 5 MINUTES

🍳 10 MINUTES

1 Break the bread into pieces, combine with the milk, and work with your hand until all the milk has been absorbed and the bread is soft. Add the eggs, scallions, pepper, and salt and mix well.

2 Heat about 2 tablespoons of oil in an 8-inch skillet. For each pancake place approximately 3 tablespoonfuls of batter in the hot oil. Spread the mixture with the back of a spoon so that it is about ¼ to ½ inch thick and 3 to 4 inches wide. Make 3 pancakes at a time. Cook on medium to high heat roughly 3 minutes on each side. Transfer to a platter, and serve right away or keep warm in the oven.

FRUIT BREAD PANCAKE

Follow the directions for Bread Galette, substituting the fruit and sugar for the scallions, salt, and pepper. Serve with cold sour cream and powdered sugar.

8 ounces leftover bread
1 cup milk
4 eggs, lightly beaten
2 cups fruit, such as apples or pears, cut into ¼-inch dice
2 tablespoons sugar
⅓ cup vegetable oil
Sour cream and powdered sugar to garnish

This unusual, inexpensive dish and the one that follows exemplify how good and versatile something as simple as a hard-cooked egg can be. The Eggs Jeannette are named after my mother, who used to make it regularly when I was a child. It is usually served lukewarm or at room temperature as a first course for dinner, but it is equally appropriate as a brunch, lunch, buffet, or picnic dish.

Many variations can be made on the same principle. In Eggs Jeannette the yolks are seasoned with garlic and parsley, but bits of leftovers such as shellfish, fish, or vegetables like spinach or mushrooms, as well as bits of leftover meat can be mixed with the yolks for different flavors.

6 hard-cooked eggs (see page 36)

2 tablespoons milk

2 cloves garlic, chopped fine

2 tablespoons chopped parsley leaves

¼ teaspoon salt

¼ teaspoon freshly ground black pepper

1 tablespoon oil

1 tablespoon butter

S E R V E S 6

⏲ 15 MINUTES

⏲ 10 MINUTES

1 Cut the eggs in half crosswise at the widest point. Remove the yolks and push them through a food mill fitted with the small screen. If you do not have a food mill, mash the yolks by hand, but do not use a food processor, which would make the yolks gummy and rubbery. Mix the sieved egg yolks with the milk, garlic, parsley, salt, and pepper. The mixture should be moist and hold together. Restuff the whites with the yolk mixture, reserving approximately 2 tablespoons for the sauce.

2 Heat the oil and butter in a skillet, preferably the nonstick type. When the oil and butter are hot and foaming, place the egg halves, stuffed side down, in the skillet. Fry at medium heat for about 2 minutes. They will brown beautifully on the stuffed side. (Egg whites do not brown well and get tough if cooked in the hot fat.) Remove the eggs from the skillet, and arrange them over the sauce in a platter or gratin dish. Serve lukewarm or at room temperature with crusty French bread.

EGG DRESSING

The 2 tablespoons of leftover egg-yolk mixture add texture to the dressing, which can be used like any thin, mustardy mayonnaise. Substitute 1 boiled egg for the egg-yolk mixture if the sauce is made for something other than our recipe.

Approximately 2 tablespoons leftover egg-yolk mixture

2 teaspoons Dijon-style mustard

2 teaspoons red wine vinegar

1 tablespoon water

Dash of salt

Dash of freshly ground black pepper

¼ cup vegetable oil

1 Place the first 6 ingredients in a food processor, and, with the motor on, add the oil slowly. Pour the dressing into a serving platter or gratin dish, and arrange the egg halves on top.

TO HARD-COOK EGGS: Immerse the eggs in cold or lukewarm tap water, then bring to a boil (for 6 eggs this should take about 2 minutes). Simmer gently. If the water boils too fast, the egg whites tend to get rubbery. After 8 minutes plunge the eggs into cold water to stop further cooking and to prevent the yolks from turning greenish-brown. Keep under running cold water until thoroughly cold. The yolks should still be a bit soft in the center.

Another dish made with hard-cooked eggs—just as easy and even faster than Eggs Jeannette—is Gratin of Eggs, a great favorite with children and adults alike. The ingredients for it are always at hand, so it is a real savior when unexpected guests arrive for dinner.

The gratin sauce (an onion-flavored white sauce) can be used to make gratins out of all kinds of leftovers, such as cauliflower, zucchini, or carrots. If the vegetables are not left over, they should be cooked first.

6 or 7 hard-cooked eggs (see page 36)

2 tablespoons butter

1½ cups sliced onions

1 tablespoon flour

1½ cups milk

½ teaspoon salt

¼ teaspoon freshly ground black pepper

½ cup grated Swiss cheese

S E R V E S   6

⏱ 15 MINUTES

⏱ 20 TO 25 MINUTES

1 Slice the eggs with an egg slicer or a knife and arrange them in a 4- to 6-cup gratin dish.

Melt the butter in a saucepan and, when it is hot, add the onions. Cook them over medium to high heat, stirring once in a while, for about 2½ to 3 minutes, until they sizzle and have just started to brown. Add the flour, mix well with a wooden spatula, and cook for about 30 seconds. Add the milk, salt, and pepper. Stirring constantly to prevent lumps, bring the mixture to a boil. Lower the heat and let the sauce simmer gently for about a minute. Pour it over the eggs.

2 Mix the sauce and the eggs gently, sprinkle with the grated cheese, and bake in a 400-degree oven for approximately 10 to 12 minutes. Place under the broiler for about 4 or 5 minutes to make a nice brown crust. Serve immediately.

Parisienne Gnocchi are marvelous little dumplings made of *pâte à choux* dough, poached in water and finished in the oven. They can be served as a first course as well as a side dish, or as a main dish itself. There are two other types of gnocchi, one of German origin that is made with potato and poached in the same manner, and another called Roman gnocchi in France, which is made with hard-wheat semolina (the same granulated flour used to make pasta), cooked with water or milk into a mush (a type of polenta), then spread on a tray, cooled, and cut into shapes and fried or baked with cheese or tomato sauce.

Pâte à choux (also known as *choux* paste, and cream-puff paste or dough) is a fast, economical, basic dough with multiple usages. Baked small balls stuffed with ice cream are known as *profiteroles;* larger ones stuffed with whipped cream or pastry cream as cream puffs; long ones are called éclairs. Puffs shaped into a large circle are the base of the Saint-Honoré cake; built into a pyramid glued together with caramel, the puffs become the classic French wedding cake, called *croquembouche.* Paris-Brest is a cake also made of a large crown of *pâte à choux,* stuffed with praline cream. Our cream-puff fritters (page 172) are light, ethereal balls of fried *pâte à choux.* Mixed with mashed potatoes and deep-fried, *pâte à choux* becomes Dauphine potatoes, and combined with Swiss cheese and baked, it is made into Gougère, often served as a hot hors d'oeuvre. The mixture for gnocchi has fewer

1 cup water

½ teaspoon salt

⅓ teaspoon grated nutmeg

2 tablespoons (¼ stick) butter

1 cup flour

¼ cup Parmesan cheese

3 eggs

1 tablespoon butter to butter the gratin dish

1 tablespoon Parmesan cheese to sprinkle on top of the gnocchi

S E R V E S   6   T O   8

⏲ 1 0   T O   1 5   M I N U T E S

⏲ 3 0   T O   3 5   M I N U T E S

eggs than a regular *pâte à choux* dough, which takes 4 eggs to 1 cup of flour. If the gnocchi dough is too loose or eggy, the eggs will expand too much in the water and make the gnocchi mushy.

Parisienne Gnocchi are formed into dumplings, then poached in water and cooled. They can be kept at this stage in the refrigerator for a couple of days and used when needed. When ready to serve, top with cheese or with a cream or tomato sauce and bake in a buttered gratin dish. The sauce can also be served separately.

1 Place the water, salt, nutmeg, and 2 tablespoons of butter in a heavy saucepan and bring to a boil. As soon as it boils, drop the entire cup of flour into the mixture at once and mix quickly with a sturdy wooden spoon.

2 Keep stirring until the mixture forms a smooth mass that separates easily from the sides of the saucepan. Then cook and stir for about 30 seconds to a minute more to dry the mixture further.

Transfer the dough to the bowl of an electric mixer, or to a regular bowl if you plan to mix it by hand. After 5 to 10 minutes, when the mixture is a bit cooler, add the 1/4 cup Parmesan cheese and 1 egg. Mix at low speed (or by hand) until the egg is incorporated. At first the mixture will seem to separate, but keep mixing and eventually the mixture will become tight and thick. Then add the second egg and mix again until smooth. Repeat with the third egg. Cover the mixture with an oiled piece of plastic wrap and let it cool.

3 Place about 3 inches of water in a large saucepan and heat it to approximately 180 degrees. It should not boil. If the mixture boils, the dumplings will cook too fast, expand, and eventually deflate. The dumplings should poach without expanding; they will expand later in the oven.

Mold the dumplings with a teaspoon; use approximately 1½ to 2 teaspoonfuls of dough. Push the dough with your index finger into the water. Get close to the water so it does not splash.

4 A faster way to shape the gnocchi, and one that makes gnocchi that are more equal in size, is with a pastry bag fitted with a 1-inch plain tip. Fill the tube with the gnocchi dough, let the tip rest on the edge of the saucepan, and press the mixture out. Slide a knife along the tip of the tube to form small gnocchi approximately 1½ inches long.

5 Poach the gnocchi for approximately 3 minutes. They will rise to the surface when they are done. Lift the gnocchi (they will not be completely cooked inside) with a slotted spoon, and place them in a bowl of iced water to cool. They will sink to the bottom of the bowl when cool. Drain and use them right away, or refrigerate for later use.

6 Arrange the gnocchi in one layer on one or two buttered gratin dishes. They should have enough space to expand. Sprinkle with the reserved Parmesan cheese, and bake in a 350-degree oven for 25 minutes. Serve right away, before they begin to deflate. We show them here with the Boulettes of Beef (page 125) and Sauce Financière (page 126).

Gratin means "crusted." (Figuratively, *le gratin* is the "upper crust" of society in colloquial French.) A dish that goes into the oven and comes out with a crusty top—for example, onion soup with the cheese baked on top—is called either a *gratin* or a *gratinée.* Usually a gratin is fairly thin and spread out so that more surface is exposed to the heat of the oven to form a crust.

Any number of ingredients can make a crust for a gratin; cheese, bread crumbs, eggs, and a white sauce with eggs or cheese are used on different types of dishes.

Our gratin of pasta and vegetables can be made with any type of cooked pasta; leftovers are fine. To give it eye appeal, texture, and taste, blanched pieces of vegetables—carrots, celery, spinach, broccoli—are used along with leftover pieces of ham, cooked meat, or chicken. The white sauce that binds it is very thin because of the starch in the pasta, which absorbs moisture. However, you do need the sauce, even though it's light. If you use milk instead of the sauce, it will end up being too runny. (You could use a light custard—milk combined with 1 egg—in place of the sauce, if you prefer.)

Cook the pasta (unless you are using already cooked leftovers) in 3 quarts of boiling salted water until it is tender but not mushy. The time will vary, depending on the type of pasta. Drain the pasta in a colander, and rinse quickly under cold water to stop cooking; drain well.

3-4 cups cooked and drained pasta
¾ cup zucchini, cut into ½-inch dice (it is not necessary to blanch)
¾ cup diced broccoli, blanched in boiling water for 3 minutes and drained
½ cup ham, cut into ¼-inch dice
⅓ cup grated American or cheddar cheese

WHITE SAUCE

1 tablespoon butter
1 tablespoon flour
2½ cups milk
½ teaspoon salt
¼ teaspoon freshly ground black pepper

S E R V E S   6

15 MINUTES

50 TO 60 MINUTES

1 Melt the butter in a saucepan, add the flour, and cook on medium heat for about 1 minute. (Notice that the *roux* gets slightly grainy and beige.) Add the cold milk, salt, and pepper, and mix well. Bring to a boil, stirring occasionally with the whisk, being sure to go in the corners where it tends to stick. Boil for about 15 to 20 seconds.

2 In a 6-cup gratin dish, combine the cooked and drained pasta with the vegetables and ham. Pour the sauce on top. Stir the mixture with a fork so that the sauce mixes with the pasta, and sprinkle with the grated cheese.

3 Bake in a 400-degree oven for about 40 to 45 minutes until the mixture is puffy and nicely browned. Serve right away.

GRATIN OF PASTA WITH VEGETABLES

PASTA CAKE

Another good dish to make from leftover pasta is a pan-fried pasta cake, a very crunchy, crisp pancake. Served with a salad, it makes a nice lunch. This recipe serves 2 to 3.

3 tablespoons vegetable oil
1 tablespoon butter
3 cups leftover cooked pasta (shells or other type), drained well
2 tablespoons chopped parsley
¼ teaspoon salt
¼ teaspoon freshly ground black pepper
1 egg, lightly beaten

1 Place the oil and butter into a 7- to 8-inch diameter skillet (preferably a nonstick type), and when the mixture is hot, add the drained pasta. Sauté the pasta for about 1 minute, stirring to coat it well with the fat. Cook on medium to high heat without stirring for about 7 to 8 minutes so that a crust forms underneath.

Mix together the parsley, salt and pepper, and egg and pour the mixture on top of the pasta. Do not stir. Let the egg fill in the spaces between the pieces of pasta and set sufficiently so that it holds the mixture together.

2 Flip the pancake over to cook the other side, or slide it onto a plate and back into the skillet. Cook for another 5 to 6 minutes so that it is nicely browned on both sides. Slide it onto a plate, and serve immediately.

Soufflés are exceptionally inexpensive and always appealing. Savory soufflés—like this one made with lettuce and cheese—can be served as a first course for a dinner or as a main course for a light brunch.

Souffler in French means to inflate, to blow, which is a fitting description of this famous concoction. It is simply a white sauce (or a purée of vegetables or fruit) that's been seasoned and combined with egg yolks and beaten egg whites. The air bubbles in the whites expand during baking, making the soufflé rise.

The whites should be beaten last because they get grainy in a matter of seconds once you stop beating, unless you add sugar or combine at once with the soufflé base to stabilize the mixture. Once combined, the mixture should be placed in the mold and either baked immediately or refrigerated in the mold for up to an hour. It can go directly from refrigerator to oven.

Soufflés do not have to be cooked in special soufflé molds. Any dish with straight sides that can go into the oven, such as the gratin dish shown here, can be used for a soufflé. In fact, the shallow gratin-type dish gives you more crust on top and bottom and produces a soufflé that's easier to divide and serve, and less likely to split. A gratin dish with a 6-cup capacity is a good size. The smaller the soufflé, the easier it is to make and serve. Twelve cups is about maximum size.

2 tablespoons butter

1 cup sliced scallions

8 cups 2-inch slices iceberg lettuce

⅓ cup water

8 tablespoons (1 stick) butter

5 tablespoons flour

1½ cups milk

5 egg yolks

¼ teaspoon Tabasco

1 teaspoon salt

2 cups grated Cheddar cheese (approximately 6 ounces)

7 egg whites

1 tablespoon dry bread crumbs or grated Parmesan cheese

Approximately 12 small strips of Cheddar cheese for decoration

S E R V E S   6   T O   8

⊍ 2 0   T O   2 5   M I N U T E S

⌂ 4 0   T O   4 5   M I N U T E S

1 Melt the butter in a large skillet and add the scallions. Sauté for about 1 minute, then add the lettuce and the water. Cover and let cook for 2 to 3 minutes. The lettuce will wilt. Uncover the wilted lettuce and let it cook on high heat until all of the liquid is evaporated. It should be practically dry.

2 For the white sauce, melt the butter in a saucepan, add the flour and mix well. Cook on medium heat for 1 minute. The mixture should be light brown and slightly grainy. Add the milk and bring to a boil, stirring. Place the palm of your hand on top of the handle of the whisk to slide it into the corners, where the sauce has a tendency to stick and burn. Keep cooking until it comes to a boil. It will get very thick.

3 Add the egg yolks, Tabasco, and salt; mix fast and thoroughly. The mixture should be yellow and fairly thick. Add the cheese and the wilted greens and mix well. Set aside.

Butter a gratin dish, add flour, shake it around well, and pour the excess flour back into the flour container.

4 Preheat oven to 375 degrees. Place the egg whites in a copper bowl and beat. You will notice that the whites cling to the top of the whisk. To make them liquid, beat very fast for 10 to 15 seconds, then slow down and continue to beat, trying to lift all the whites with the whisk as you beat. Don't go too fast at first, but be sure that the mixture is agitated all the time. When one hand tires, use the other for a few seconds. Increase the speed as the whites get fluffy. It should take 2 to 3½ minutes for the egg whites to firm and hold a peak. (Notice the long peak at the end of the whisk as well as in the bowl.) The egg whites should be glossy and tight in texture without either weeping or being dry.

5 Add about a quarter of the egg whites to the white sauce, stirring fast with the whisk. This lightens the white sauce so that the rest of the whites can be folded in easily. Give the remaining egg whites a few strokes with the large whisk to eliminate any graininess. Then fold the whites into the base with a large rubber spatula.

6 Pour into the prepared mold and smooth the top with a spatula. Run the side of your thumb around the edge of the dish to make it clean and loose so that the soufflé doesn't stick to the edge while cooking. Sprinkle with the bread crumbs or Parmesan cheese.

Decorate the top of the soufflé, making a crisscross pattern with the cheese strips.

7 Bake for 15 minutes, then reduce to 350 degrees and cook for another 25 minutes. Serve immediately.

LEFTOVERS: Here are two of my favorite ways of using leftover soufflé. Both make a very nice first course.

GRATIN SOUFFLÉ

1 Cut the leftover soufflé into strips and arrange on a buttered gratin dish. For approximately half the original recipe, sprinkle with ⅓ cup of grated cheese and ⅓ cup of milk.

2 Place under the broiler in the middle of the oven, so it is not too close to the broiler, and bake for about 10 minutes. The gratin will brown and puff. Serve immediately.

COLD SOUFFLÉ VINAIGRETTE

2 teaspoons Dijon mustard

1 tablespoon white vinegar

Dash of salt and freshly ground pepper

⅓ cup vegetable oil

¼ cup chopped basil or parsley

1 For another variation, serve the soufflé cold, sliced, and arranged on a platter with herbs and vinaigrette. Pour the dressing on top of the sliced soufflé, and decorate the center with basil or parsley. To make the vinaigrette, combine mustard, vinegar, salt, and pepper. Mix well and slowly add the oil. Add basil or parsley.

THE PROBLEM SOUFFLÉ

A less than perfect soufflé can be made more than presentable by unmolding it and inverting it onto a plate. To unmold, use the tip of a knife or your fingers to pry the soufflé away from the edges, loosening it all around. Serve in wedges and accompany with a tomato sauce such as the one that follows. This slightly grainy, beautifully red sauce has a very fresh taste. It's quite good served with pasta, too.

TOMATO SAUCE

2 tablespoons olive oil
¾ cup chopped onions
4 cups chopped fresh tomatoes
½ teaspoon dried oregano
1 teaspoon salt
½ teaspoon freshly ground black pepper

1 Heat the oil in a saucepan and add the onions. Sauté for 2 minutes on medium heat. Then add the rest of the ingredients. Cover, and cook on medium heat for about 10 minutes.

2 Push through a food mill, using the large screen.

3 Spoon over the unmolded soufflé or serve separately.

EXTRA SOUFFLÉ MIXTURE: Egg whites sometimes give you more volume than other times. If you find you have extra soufflé mixture, simply bake it in a small buttered soufflé mold.

BEATING EGG WHITES: Eggs beaten in an unlined copper bowl, cleaned with vinegar and salt or copper polish, have a nice spongy texture that's good for a soufflé. There is a chemical reaction between the copper bowl and the egg whites that lowers the pH or acidifies the whites and gives the beaten egg whites a better texture. A few drops of lemon juice or a dash of salt or a bit of cream of tartar should be added to acidify the egg whites if you are not using a copper bowl. In any event, don't use an aluminum bowl—it will blacken egg whites and prevent them from expanding.

I prefer to beat egg whites by hand because in an electric mixer the whisk follows a path without any deviation and a portion of the whites doesn't get mixed at all times. This can make the whites grainy. This is especially true for small quantities. If the quantity is large, that part which doesn't get mixed in is proportionately smaller and doesn't affect the result.

If you do beat the egg whites by machine, finish them by hand. Use a large flexible balloon whisk and a 12- to 14-inch bowl.

TEMPERATURE AND THE EGG WHITES: Use eggs right from the refrigerator. Cold contracts, so that if your whites are cold they'll beat into very small, tight bubbles that hold well.

Lukewarm egg whites give you greater volume but make a mixture that may get too airy and break down, making the soufflé split and collapse. (One exception is if you use eggs fresh from a farm, which are high in albumin and can be beaten at room temperature without breaking down.)

This inexpensive pâté can be prepared quickly, although it needs 10 to 12 hours in the refrigerator to set. It yields enough for about 60 toasts.

This is a precooked pâté. The cooked ingredients are combined into what is sometimes called a *mousse,* meaning "foam" in French, something that is beaten to produce an emulsion and a light texture. Dishes combined with whipped cream or beaten egg whites often take the name of *mousse,* such as chocolate mousse or scallop, or chicken liver mousse, akin to this pâté.

This pâté, made with uncooked butter, is lighter and more digestible than one made with pork or chicken fat and cooked. It is important to respect the proportion of fat to liver. Excess liver makes the pâté dark, strong, bitter, and grainy. Be sure that the livers are free of sinews and of any part that is green, which indicates that some of the bitter bile has been in contact with the liver. Pale yellow livers tend to have a mellow, rich taste and are preferable to deep red ones (see page 104 for more information).

Pâtés usually do not freeze well, especially coarse country pâtés. The inside becomes watery and grainy. Because of its extra-smooth and compact texture, however, this chicken liver pâté freezes perfectly. Do not freeze with the aspic or decoration. To freeze, cover tightly with plastic wrap, then aluminum foil. Defrost it slowly under refrigeration for 24 to 48 hours before decorating and glazing. Small soufflé molds are

1 pound chicken livers

⅔ cup thinly sliced onions

1 clove garlic, peeled and crushed (½ teaspoon)

2 bay leaves, crushed

¼ teaspoon thyme leaves

1 cup water

2 teaspoons salt

1½ cups (3 sticks) butter, softened

Freshly ground black pepper

2 teaspoons Cognac or Scotch whisky

A piece of tomato skin and green of scallion for decoration (optional)

1 envelope unflavored gelatin for aspic (optional)

S E R V E S   1 2   T O   1 4

15 TO 20 MINUTES

15 TO 30 MINUTES
FOR DECORATION

ideal for freezing because they can be defrosted in only a couple of hours.

The decoration and the aspic glaze, though optional, raise a fairly ordinary preparation to the level of an elegant, classic dish. The aspic sets the decoration, keeping it from curling and wilting, but you can decorate the pâté without glazing with aspic if you serve the pâté soon after it's decorated. There are some basic rules of decorating which you should observe. The decorations should be edible, such as green scallion and red tomato. Avoid vegetables that are bitter, such as lemon peel, or those, such as beets, which will discolor the food. Use carrots, tomatoes, olives, and different shades of green from leeks or lettuce. Cut the vegetables very thin; blanch them in boiling water for a few seconds to make more pliable.

1 Place the livers, onions, garlic, bay leaves, thyme, water, and 1 teaspoon salt in a saucepan. Bring to a boil, cover, and cook at a bare simmer for 7 to 8 minutes. Remove from the heat and let the mixture sit for about 5 minutes.

Take out the solids with a slotted spoon and place them in the bowl of a food processor with metal blade. (Reserve and strain the liquid to make the aspic.) Start processing the liver, adding the butter piece by piece. Finally, add the second teaspoon salt, the pepper, and Cognac or whisky and process for 2 more minutes so that the mixture is very creamy and completely smooth. If the mixture looks broken down, with visible fat, let it cool in the refrigerator for about 1 hour to harden the butter, then process again until the mixture is creamy and smooth.

Pour into a mold. Decorate or refrigerate to set and serve as is.

TO DECORATE

1 Blanch the piece of scallion in boiling water for 10 to 15 seconds until it wilts, then cool it under cold water. The blanching flattens it and makes it pliable, and the cold water sets the color and prevents yellowing.

Lay it flat on the table, and pat it dry with paper towels. Cut some strips from the leaves, and arrange them on the border of the pâté to make a "frame" for the decoration.

Cut some leaves into pointed, thin strips to make stems. Arrange them on top of the pâté, and set them by pressing with the tip of your fingers or the point of a knife.

2 Use different sizes of leaves and shades of green. Fold some of the larger "leaves," make others into long stems, and some into tiny lozenges. Use your imagination; there are no rules for this part.

3 Place a tiny bit of green at the end of each stem to make a calyx for the flower. Cut small pieces of tomato skin with jagged edges to suggest flowers, and place them at the ends of the stems.

4 Use the small trimmings to make the willowlike wildflower. One small piece of tomato skin is enough for the whole pâté. Refrigerate the pâté while you prepare the aspic.

5 To make the aspic, combine the strained cup of liquid from the liver and the gelatin in a saucepan. Stir gently over heat until the mixture almost comes to a boil and the gelatin is completely melted. Place the saucepan on ice, and stir until the liquid becomes very syrupy. At this stage the aspic is shiny and glistening, and about to set. This is the right moment to use it. If it becomes too hard, remelt it and start again.

6 Take the pâté out of the refrigerator, and pour and spread 3 or 4 tablespoons of aspic on top. The layer of aspic should be approximately ¼ inch thick. The aspic sets the decor, prevents it from drying out, and gives the effect of a beautiful stained-glass window. To serve, scoop out about a teaspoonful of pâté and place it on each plate with a bit of aspic and some Melba toast (recipe follows).

7 The mixture can also be prepared in small soufflé molds of about ½-cup capacity, each one decorated differently.

MELBA TOAST: Escoffier invented this toast for the famous opera singer Nellie Melba, as he did the Peach Melba.

1 Toast thin-sliced bread in the toaster. As soon as it comes out of the toaster, trim the slices on all four sides. Slide your knife into the soft area between the bottom and top crusts and separate the bread into two extremely thin layers. It is not necessary to toast the white side. This is the only way you can make really good thin toast: by toasting a thicker slice, then splitting it in half after it has been toasted. If you tried to toast an extra-thin slice it would curl and burn rather than brown.

Fried vegetables are always welcome at our table. Zucchini flowers make a perfect first course in summer, and my family considers fried eggplant, soup, salad, and cheese to be a fine dinner.

Here we dip eggplant into a tempura-style batter made of flour, egg yolk, and ice-cold water. We are fond of this tempura batter and use it to fry all sorts of vegetables. We often shred a mixture of vegetables—carrots, zucchini, parsley, broccoli, cauliflower, scallions, and the like—stir them into the tempura batter, then fry them in large spoonfuls in oil, like the shredded apples in beer batter on page 141. (The apple fritter batters can be used for the eggplants, too. In fact, all the batters are interchangeable, though they each have a distinct taste and texture.)

Instructions for a second method of frying eggplant—this one without batter—follow on the next page.

4 to 6 very thin eggplants (about 1½ inches in diameter) or 2 to 3 larger eggplants split in half lengthwise (about 2 pounds)

1⅓ cups flour

2 egg yolks

1⅓ cups ice-cold water

Oil for deep frying

S E R V E S   4   T O   6

⏱ 1 0   M I N U T E S

🍲 8   T O   1 0   M I N U T E S

1 Slice the eggplants into ¼-inch slices, leaving the slices attached at one end. Small eggplant can be sliced whole; large eggplant should be cut in half. Press down on the eggplant to fan out the slices. This fan shape looks beautiful on the plate, but it also exposes the maximum surface area to the oil. Consequently, it doesn't take very long to cook. There's no need to salt batter-fried eggplant, as the batter assures you a crisp crust.

Place flour, egg yolks, and half the water in a bowl and work with a whisk until the mixture is smooth (see page 180). Whisk in the rest of the water. This batter produces a very crisp, thin coating. The batter can be made with a whole egg rather than the egg yolks but either way make sure the water is ice cold. If it's not cold it never seems to get as crisp as it could.

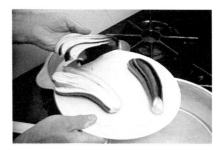

2 Heat approximately ½ inch of oil in a large skillet until very hot. Dip the eggplant fans in the batter. The batter is quite runny and not too much will adhere to the eggplant.

3 Place each piece flat in the hot oil and cook on medium to high heat for about 4 to 5 minutes on one side. Turn and cook another 3 minutes. The fans should be nice and brown and cooked through. If your skillet is not large enough to accommodate several eggplants, make them in batches or use several skillets.

When done, remove to a cookie sheet lined with paper towels, and sprinkle with salt.

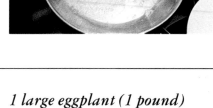

FLOUR-DREDGED FRIED EGGPLANT

1 Cut the eggplant into slices about ⅜ to ½ inch thick (approximately 10 slices) and sprinkle them with salt on both sides. Arrange the slices on a cookie sheet with another cookie sheet on top and add a weight (such as a food processor or a mixer) to press down on the eggplant. Let the slices drain for 30 minutes. The salting and pressing cure the eggplant, remove some of the bitterness, and prevent the slices from absorbing too much fat during cooking.

Drain the slices and dry with paper towels, then dip into flour. Pat the slices gently so that not too much flour stays on them.

1 large eggplant (1 pound)

Salt

Approximately ½ cup flour for the dipping

Approximately 1 cup vegetable oil

2 Heat about ¼ inch of oil in a skillet and place the slices in the hot oil. Cook approximately 2 minutes on each side. No salt is added to the slices at the end because of the curing.

One large eggplant should serve 3.

T his dish is usually served as a vegetable course, but it can also be served as a first course. It is good reheated, and left over, it can be used in a soup or stew. To enrich it, add little pieces of leftover meat, such as ham, sausage, or roast, as well as pieces of other vegetables. Use white cabbage or savoy cabbage, which is leafier.

1 2½-pound head cabbage

2 cups water

1 teaspoon salt

¼ teaspoon freshly ground black pepper

3 tablespoons butter

½ cup grated Swiss cheese

⅔ cup fresh bread crumbs

S E R V E S   6   T O   8

🥣 5   T O   1 0   M I N U T E S

⏱ 4 5   M I N U T E S

1 Cut the cabbage in half, remove the core, and cut the cabbage across into ½-inch slices.
Place the shredded cabbage in a pot, preferably stainless steel, and add the 2 cups of water. Bring to a boil, cover, and simmer for about 20 minutes. By then the cabbage should be wilted and soft, but still a bit firm, and most of the water should have evaporated. If any water is left, keep cooking with the lid off until no water is visible and the cabbage is just moist.

2 Pour into a gratin dish and sprinkle with the salt, pepper, butter, and Swiss cheese. Sprinkle with bread crumbs and place in a 400-degree oven for 25 minutes.

Almost any green can be stewed for a very fast and appealing vegetable dish. Here we are stewing kale, but escarole and spinach are excellent made this way. Spinach cooks in 1 minute; escarole, 2 to 3 minutes; and the kale takes 8 to 10 minutes, depending on how young and tender it is. Sometimes I make it with rape or broccoli rabe (a type of bitter broccoli) and serve it cold sprinkled with olive oil and pimentos.

Approximately 12 cups lightly packed, clean kale leaves

½ cup vegetable or olive oil

2 cloves garlic, peeled, crushed, and chopped fine (1 teaspoon)

¼ teaspoon hot pepper flakes

1 teaspoon salt

1½ cups water

S E R V E S   6

⊙ 5   M I N U T E S

⊙ 2 0   M I N U T E S

1 Remove the center rib of the kale leaves, if tough; it can be left in if the kale is tender and young.

Heat the oil, garlic, and pepper flakes in a large saucepan and cook for 1 minute on medium heat until the garlic sizzles and starts to brown. Add the kale, salt, and water. Cover, bring to a boil, and cook on medium to high heat for about 8 to 10 minutes. The water should be practically gone. If the water evaporates too fast during cooking, add some so the kale stays moist. If there is still too much water in it after 10 minutes, keep boiling uncovered until the rest of the water evaporates. The kale should be moist with no liquid left. It can be served hot or at room temperature.

H E R B E D   Z U C C H I N I

W hen you buy zucchini, choose long, firm, and shiny specimens. They should break when twisted or bent. Long, narrow ones have fewer seeds. If the inside is very soft and cottony, remove it. Zucchini is good in salad, cooked or raw, excellent in gratins, in soups—or sautéed, as in our recipe.

3 zucchini (1½ pounds)

¼ cup vegetable oil

1 tablespoon minced chives

½ teaspoon salt

⅛ teaspoon freshly ground black pepper

1 tablespoon butter

1 piece tomato skin cut into little strips for decoration

S E R V E S   6

5 MINUTES

5 MINUTES

1 Cut the zucchini lengthwise into slices ¼ inch thick. Stack the slices and cut them into ¼-inch strips, about 2½ inches long. You should have approximately 7 cups.

Heat the oil in one large or two small skillets. When it is hot, add the zucchini. It shouldn't be layered more than ½ inch thick so it will steam and soften without browning. Sauté on high heat for 4½ to 5 minutes. Add the chives, salt, pepper, and butter and mix well. The zucchini should be soft and a bit transparent, but not soggy.

2 At serving time, transfer to a serving dish and sprinkle with the pieces of tomato skin to decorate.

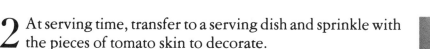

This is an ideal dish to serve when unexpected guests arrive or when you need a "filler" to complete a family meal. There is only a slight drawback to it: It should be eaten immediately after it is cooked, when it is most savory and crisp. Leftovers can be crisped under the broiler, but they are never as good as when they have just come out of the skillet.

In this recipe the potatoes are shredded into little strips, although they could also be grated like the onions to give a different texture and taste. If you make the batter ahead, refrigerate it, covered tightly with a piece of plastic wrap, to lessen discoloration. The top of the batter will discolor anyway, but as you stir it the discoloration will disappear, and it doesn't change the taste. Don't prepare the batter more than a few hours ahead or it will become watery.

1 large or 2 medium onions (to make ½ cup grated onions)

3 to 4 large potatoes (1¾ pounds), peeled

3 eggs

2 tablespoons flour

⅓ cup chopped parsley

1 teaspoon salt

½ teaspoon freshly ground black pepper

1 cup vegetable oil (corn or cottonseed)

YIELD: 12 TO 14 PANCAKES

⊘ 10 TO 15 MINUTES

⊘ 12 TO 15 MINUTES

1 Peel the onions and grate them with a hand grater. Use the small side of the grater that seems to have been perforated with nails. These tiny holes abrade in any direction and liquefy the onions to a smooth purée.

2 Shred the potatoes on the side of the grater where you usually grate cheese. These longer, oblong holes cut in one direction only, downward. Hold the potato with the palm of your hand only, to avoid cutting your fingertips.

   Place the shredded potatoes (you should have about 3 cups) in a towel. Twist the towel with one hand and press with the other to extrude the juice. Most of the starch is released with the juice, so that pancakes will be airy, crisp, and not starchy.

3 Combine all the other ingredients except the oil in a bowl, preferably stainless steel to prevent discoloration, and mix thoroughly. The batter will be fairly loose.

4 Heat 2 to 3 tablespoons of the vegetable oil in a skillet, preferably nonstick. (These pancakes do not absorb much oil, so this amount of oil is enough to fry several batches.) For each pancake, place about 3 tablespoonfuls of the mixture in the skillet. (In an 8-inch diameter pan we were able to fry 3 at a time.) Spread the mixture right away with the back of the spoon so that the pancakes are very thin, with little holes in the center. Fry on medium to high heat for a good minute and a half to 2 minutes on each side. The potatoes should be thin and crispy. Use a large spatula to flip them over.

5 Remove with the spatula. Notice that the edges are jagged and quite crisp. Serve as soon as possible.

This is an unusual and highly flavored coleslaw. It can be made with white or red cabbage or, as we have done, with both, seasoned separately and then combined.

This cabbage salad can also be made with iceberg lettuce or any other crunchy, slightly tough salad green such as escarole or curly endive (chicory). The advantage of cabbage is that it does not wilt as fast as lettuce, so it can be prepared an hour or so ahead.

---

9 cups shredded red or white cabbage (approximately one small head), or half red and half white

---

4 or 5 cloves garlic, peeled, crushed, and chopped very fine (1 tablespoon)

---

1 two-ounce can anchovy fillets

---

1 tablespoon wine vinegar

½ cup olive oil or vegetable oil

½ teaspoon freshly ground black pepper

½ teaspoon salt

S E R V E S   6

⏱ 1 2 T O 1 5 M I N U T E S

1 Cut the cabbage in half and remove the core. Cut across with a long knife into ¼-inch slices. (In a professional kitchen, the electric ham slicer is used to shred the cabbage.)

Crush and chop the garlic and anchovy fillets into a purée. Stir the purée into the vinegar, oil, pepper, and salt. Do not make the sauce in a food processor, because it will thicken too much, like a mayonnaise, and will cling to the cabbage, "dirtying" it. You want a transparent dressing, the consistency of a vinaigrette, that makes the cabbage glossy and enhances the color and shape of the salad. Mix the sauce with the cabbage.

2 If you use both red and white cabbage, mix them with the dressing in separate bowls. Place the red cabbage in a pretty glass or crystal bowl, and make a well in the center to form a nest. Mound the white cabbage in the center. Decorate all around with little sprigs of parsley, and in the center place a rose made of a strip of tomato skin rolled into a scroll.

In French cooking, *à la Grecque* refers to different types of vegetables cooked with lemon or vinegar, oil, and coriander and served cold. These marinated vegetables are made ahead because they improve in flavor in the refrigerator. They will keep at least 1 week refrigerated, and are ideal for buffets and to serve as a first course or to mix with a green salad.

The vegetables should be cooked briefly to retain some crunchiness. Mushrooms, artichoke bottoms, cauliflower, and even zucchini are often prepared in this manner. The dish can be prepared any time of year, because there are always vegetables in season that are excellent made *à la Grecque.* This carrot and onion mixture is attractive, inexpensive, and flavorful.

1 pound carrots, peeled (6 or 7 carrots)

1½ pounds large white or yellow onions (5 or 6 onions)

½ cup dry white wine

¼ cup vinegar

½ cup water

⅓ cup oil, preferably olive oil

½ teaspoon whole black peppercorns

1 teaspoon coriander seeds

½ teaspoon dried thyme

½ teaspoon fennel seeds

2 teaspoons salt

3 bay leaves

¼ teaspoon freshly ground black pepper

¼ cup oil, preferably olive oil, to add to the salad at the end

SERVES 6 TO 8

15 MINUTES

12 TO 15 MINUTES

1 Cut the carrots into 2-inch segments, and each segment into sticks about ⅜ inch thick. Peel the onions and cut into sixths. Separate each section into layers. You should have approximately 3 cups of carrots and 6 cups of onions.

   Place all the ingredients except the onions and ¼ cup of oil in a large saucepan, and bring to a boil. Cover and boil for about 6 minutes. Add the onions, bring to a boil, and simmer for another 3 to 4 minutes. The carrots should be a bit soft but still crunchy, and the onions should be firm.

2 Pour the vegetables with the broth into a bowl and let cool. Stir in the reserved oil. Serve cool with crunchy French bread.

MARINATED PEPPERS

This is a very useful concoction to have on hand. It keeps well in the refrigerator and it can be used in many different ways. We make it often as it's a favorite of my wife, who has it for lunch, spread on a slice of toasted French bread, maybe with a few anchovy fillets on top. It is ideal served as an antipasto or as a garnish. It supplies color and flavor when mixed into a green salad, bean salad, or potato salad.

Fleshy, round sweet peppers are excellent for this dish. They come in green, red, and yellow, but yellow ones are rarely available, and red ones appear on the market in summer only. The taste of all three is basically the same. Avoid buying soft, wilted, or wrinkled peppers. Look for shiny, plump ones with thick flesh. The long, tapered, pale green peppers—so-called Italian peppers—are sweet and also excellent for this recipe.

Removing the skin greatly improves the dish. Roasting the peppers to release the skin partially cooks them and makes them more tender and sweet. Removing the tough skin imparts delicacy and removes bitterness from the peppers. Peeled peppers can also be stuffed with a mixture of rice and meat and baked in the oven to be served hot or cold.

We used a tomato in the following recipe, mostly to give color and replace the red peppers which were not available.

3 thick, roundish green peppers (12 to 14 ounces)

3 long Italian peppers (7 to 8 ounces)

1 ripe, red tomato

3 to 4 cloves garlic, peeled, crushed, and chopped very fine (1 tablespoon)

⅓ cup olive or vegetable oil

1 teaspoon salt

½ teaspoon freshly ground black pepper

SERVES 6
⏰ 30 MINUTES

1 Roast the peppers on a rack under the broiler, about 1 inch away from the flame, for approximately 12 minutes, turning them every 4 minutes or so until they are black, charred, and blistered all over. Immediately enclose them in a plastic bag and let them steam for 10 minutes. The steam releases the skin, making it very easy to slide the skin off. Pull the skin off; it will release easily.

2 Split the peppers in half. Remove the stem and scrape out the seeds. Cut into ½-inch strips. You should have approximately 2½ cups of strips.

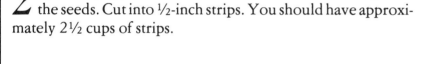

3 Peel the tomato (see Tomato Salad with Basil, page 73). Cut it in half crosswise and press it to extrude the seeds. (The seeds and skin can be saved for stock.) Cut the flesh into ¼- to ½-inch dice and mix with the pepper. Add the garlic, oil, salt, and pepper, and mix well. The mixture can be kept in the refrigerator for 1 to 2 weeks. Serve with crunchy French bread.

The ingredients for this salad, and the one that follows, are available year round. Both salads improve and develop in flavor in the refrigerator, especially cucumber salad, and can be kept for several days. They make a handy first course for dinner, or a snack for lunch, or a nice filler for sandwiches, alone or mixed with cold cuts, bacon, or cheese.

The mild carrot salad is excellent with cheese and bread, particularly a Gorgonzola and a black pumpernickel. Try to get carrots that aren't too woody in the center, which they tend to be in winter.

3 to 4 large carrots, peeled (approximately ¾ pound)

½ cup walnut pieces (or other nuts)

½ cup coarsely chopped parsley

1½ teaspoons salt

1 teaspoon coarsely ground black pepper

1 tablespoon wine vinegar

⅓ cup vegetable oil

S E R V E S   6

⏱ 1 0 T O 1 2 M I N U T E S

1 Using a hand grater, grate the carrots on the side with the large holes. Keep the carrot flat and try to hold it with the palm of your hand as you push down. Be careful not to cut your fingers. At the end, use a knife to cut the pieces that you cannot grate, and add them to the salad or use them for stock. Combine all the ingredients, tossing so the carrots are thoroughly impregnated with the seasonings. Eat cool, but not cold. The delicate taste of the salad will be overpowered if served cold. Serve on a lettuce leaf.

This cucumber salad, a recipe of my father-in-law, Louis Augier, is a great favorite at our house. Here is my version. Even without "Grandpa's touch" the recipe is excellent.

Cucumbers should be firm and preferably fairly long and narrow; so-called English cucumbers are very good. When they are thick and heavy, they tend to be very seedy.

4 to 5 cucumbers (approximately 2 pounds)

2 large sweet onions, peeled and sliced very thin (2 cups)

1 tablespoon salt

4 tablespoons distilled white vinegar

2 tablespoons vegetable oil

2 teaspoons sugar

½ teaspoon salt, if needed

S E R V E S   6

🕐 3 5   M I N U T E S

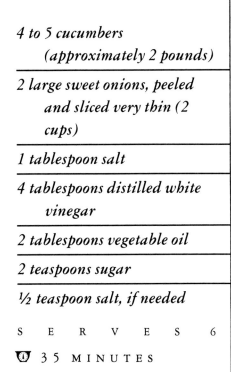

1 Peel the cucumbers and cut in halves. Seed them with a teaspoon. Cut into thin slices (no more than ⅓ inch thick). You should have 5 cups.

Toss with the sliced onion and the tablespoon of salt. Drain the mixture in a colander for half an hour.

Rinse the cucumbers briefly, then press them gently through fingers to extrude most of the water. Place in a bowl, and combine with the vinegar, oil, sugar, and a bit of extra salt if needed. Macerate, or serve right away.

2 For a nice presentation serve in a tomato basket . To make the basket: Follow the curve of the tomato and cut 3 separate strips by slicing vertically. Stop three-quarters of the way down, leaving the strips attached at the base of the tomato. Then take a small knife and, holding it horizontally, cut the loose part from the center of the tomato and remove. [Clockwise from top: a tomato basket; Cucumber Salad served in a tomato basket; Carrot and Walnut Salad.]

In summer, large, soft tomatoes contain a lot of liquid. To partially drain, sprinkle the cut tomatoes with salt and allow them to stand for 10 to 15 minutes, then pour off the liquid. Removing the skins, juice, and seeds is optional, however; the tomatoes are good both ways.

In the following recipe the tomatoes are sliced and served with very thinly sliced onions, oil, and vinegar. In the next recipe, the tomatoes are seeded, peeled, cut into cubes, then simply combined with fresh basil and dressing. The first goes a little further, serving 6 rather than 4.

3 to 4 large, ripe tomatoes (approximately 1½ pounds)

1 large onion, peeled and cut crosswise into ⅛-inch-thick slices

1 teaspoon salt

½ teaspoon freshly ground black pepper

2 tablespoons wine vinegar

4 tablespoons olive oil or vegetable oil

2 to 3 tablespoons whole parsley leaves

S E R V E S 6

🕐 20 MINUTES

1 Slice the tomatoes across their width into ⅜-inch slices with an extremely sharp knife, especially if they are very ripe. Arrange the slices, overlapping slightly, on a large oval or round serving platter.

2 Separate the rings of the onion slices and place them on top of the tomatoes. Sprinkle the salt on top, and leave to macerate for about 15 minutes. Then, holding the tomatoes with a plate or with your hands, pour out the extra liquid. Sprinkle with pepper, vinegar, oil, and finally the parsley (flat parsley is especially good). Serve cool or at room temperature. The salad should not be ice cold.

There is nothing as good as a fresh tomato salad with tomatoes still warm from the garden. And nothing complements tomatoes as well as fresh basil and olive oil. It's too bad good tomatoes are so hard to get in the winter.

3 to 4 large, ripe, red tomatoes (approximately 1½ pounds)

1 teaspoon salt

½ teaspoon freshly ground black pepper

1 tablespoon wine vinegar

2 tablespoons vegetable or olive oil

⅓ cup fresh basil leaves

S E R V E S   4

10 TO 15 MINUTES

1 Impale each tomato on a fork, and roast it for 10 to 15 seconds over a gas flame. Using a knife, pull off the skin—it will release easily. Or drop the tomatoes into boiling water for a few seconds, cool them in cold water, and peel them. The latter method is particularly efficient when you have a large number of tomatoes, which makes boiling a whole pot of water worthwhile. Cut the tomatoes in half crosswise, and squeeze out the seeds. (Keep the skin and liquid for stock.) Then cut into ½-inch cubes and combine them with the salt, pepper, vinegar, and oil in a serving bowl.

2 Stack the basil leaves, fold them, and cut them into a fine julienne (called *chiffonnade*). Mix with the tomatoes. Decorate the center with a sprig of fresh basil and serve.

THE MAIN DISH

FISH AND SHELLFISH

Sautéed Whiting Grenoble Style

Roe and Liver Persillade

Fish Fillets Niçoise

Mackerel in Vinaigrette

Mayonnaise of Fish

Timbales of Fish

Pilaff of Mussels / Mussels Provençal

CHICKEN

Stew of Chicken Wings / Rice Pancake

Chicken Cassoulet / Boston Lettuce Salad

Tureens of Cassoulet

Chicken in Mustard Sauce

Chicken Livers Sautéed with Vinegar

Mayonnaise of Chicken

MEATS

Sausage and Potato Stew / Escarole Salad with Garlic Dressing

Stuffed Breast of Lamb

Navarin of Lamb

Roast Lamb Breast Provençal / Onions in Papillote

Potato Ragoût

Gratin Parmentier

Boulettes of Beef / Sauce Financière

When you buy a fish, make sure that the scales are shiny and firmly attached to the body. The eyes should be clear and the gills should have a nice pink color. In general, the flesh should be firm. It is best to go to a fish store where the fish are displayed whole so that you can recognize freshness. It is fairly difficult to determine freshness when you look at the fillet only.

A fish out of the water for a few hours does not have a fishy smell; it has practically no smell at all, or only the fresh smell of seawater or seaweed. When a fish has a "fishy taste," it is not fresh. Some fish tastes stronger than others. A fatty fish, such as bluefish or mackerel, is stronger than porgy or whiting.

If it is absolutely impossible to buy fresh fish where you live, buy the thickest possible fish. The thicker the piece of fish, the better it keeps in the freezing process. If possible, buy frozen whole fish, such as trout or salmon, rather than fillets. In any case, be sure to defrost the well-wrapped fish slowly under refrigeration, if you have time. For a faster method, place it in cold water. It should not lose too much moisture in defrosting so that the end result is moist.

Whiting is one of the most under-rated fish. Its flesh is extremely moist and delicate, and it is very easy to eat, because the skeleton is quite simple, consisting of a large triangular central bone with practically no others. The white flesh is mild, moist, and tasty. Other good inexpensive fish can be used for this recipe, such as hake, porgy, croaker, cod, sea perch, and scrod.

To cook something Grenoble style (usually a piece of fish) means to sauté it in a skillet and garnish it with sautéed bread crumbs, little cubes of lemon flesh, capers, and parsley. We have replaced the capers (which are expensive) with small bits of sweet red pepper to add color and taste.

It is important before you sauté a fish to pat it dry. Dredge it in flour, then shake off excess flour. Do not crowd the skillet, and cook over a fairly high heat. If the fish is wet, the flour and water form a paste. The fish should never be floured too far in advance or the flour will get soggy. If the flour gets wet, if the skillet is crowded, or if the heat is not high enough, the fish will stick and fall apart into a mush.

We gutted the fish ourselves so that we could use the roe and the liver to make Roe and Liver Persillade (page 80).

6 whitings, 8 to 12 ounces each, ungutted (approximately 6 to 7 ounces cleaned with the heads removed)

4 slices bread

1 large lemon

3 to 4 tablespoons flour

¼ cup vegetable oil to sauté the fish

2 tablespoons butter to sauté the fish

1 teaspoon salt

¼ cup vegetable oil to sauté the bread

3 tablespoons butter to finish the dish

1 small to medium sweet red pepper, seeded and cut into ¼-inch dice (½ cup)

⅓ cup coarsely chopped parsley

SERVES 6

⏱ 30 MINUTES

🍳 10 MINUTES

1 Scale the whitings gently with a knife. The scales are not very large, but nevertheless should be removed.

2 Cut off the heads. Remove the guts and save the roe and liver for another dish (see p. 80).

3 The inside of the cavity is lined with a black skin which is bitter and has to be removed. Pull it off gently; it will come away easily.

4 To make the whiting easier to eat, remove the center bone the length of the cavity. Make a small cut along each side of the bone and slide your finger underneath. Push with your finger to get this central bone loose, and pry it out. Break it at the limit of the opening. It will come out easily.

5 Cut enough bread to make 1½ cups into ⅜-inch dice. Peel and seed the lemon and cut into ⅜-inch dice; you should have ½ cup diced fruit. (Save the lemon peel to be candied, see page 131.) Dry the fish, dredge in flour, and shake off excess.

6 Heat ¼ cup of oil and 2 tablespoons of the butter until very hot in a very large skillet or two smaller ones. Sprinkle the whitings inside and out with the salt. Place them in the skillet in alternate directions to take the utmost advantage of the space.

7 Cook for about 4 to 5 minutes on medium to high heat on one side. Turn them over and cook approximately another 4 minutes. The fish should be cooked enough so that a nice crust forms, making them easy to turn.

Heat ¼ cup of oil and sauté the bread. Move the bread around the pan constantly so that it doesn't burn but gets nicely brown all over. This will take 3 to 4 minutes on medium to high heat.

8 Arrange the cooked whitings on a large platter or on individual plates, and sprinkle them with the lemon and bread cubes.

Heat 3 tablespoons of butter in a skillet, add the pepper, and sauté for about 30 seconds. Spoon the pepper and foaming butter directly on top of the whitings, sprinkle with parsley, and serve immediately.

We all know fish roe in the form of caviar, highly priced from fish like sturgeon, less so for salmon or lumpfish. And there's fresh shad roe, considered by some a long-awaited harbinger of spring. But don't limit yourself to only these known staples. Ask your fishmonger for the long, tapered roe of flat fish, such as sole, flounder, fluke, or brill, as well as roe from other fish. The milt (the male sperm repository as opposed to the roe of the female) is also highly prized in most fish, especially herring and salmon. The fish livers, like cod livers, are good, too. The liver and milt should be cooked faster than the roe.

Clean the roe and liver of any black filaments or sinews, which are bitter. As with any other liver, make sure to remove any yellowish-green bits on top of the liver, which indicate that the gall bladder (a little sac filled with bitter liquid and attached to the liver) has broken. The bitter liquid, called bile, may also run on the flesh of the fish inside the cavity and color the flesh greenish.

1 pound roe and liver, combined, or one or the other

½ teaspoon salt

1 or 2 tablespoons flour

2 tablespoons vegetable oil

1 tablespoon butter to cook the roe and liver

2 tablespoons butter to finish the dish

1 clove garlic, peeled, crushed, and chopped very fine (½ teaspoon)

⅓ cup chopped fresh parsley

½ teaspoon lemon juice or vinegar

S E R V E S 6

⏱ 5 MINUTES

⏱ 8 TO 10 MINUTES

1 The roe on the lower right are from whitings; at the left are the livers from the whitings. The larger pieces of roe in the back are from flounder. Clean the roe and liver and pat them dry. Sprinkle with the salt and flour.

Place the oil and 1 tablespoon butter in a large skillet and when hot, place the roe flat down in the pan and cook on medium to high heat for about 4 minutes. Turn the roe with a spatula, add the liver (it does not have to brown flat like the roe), cover, lower the heat to medium, and cook another 2 to 3 minutes.

2 Arrange the roe and liver on a serving platter or individual plates. Heat the 2 tablespoons of butter in the skillet, and add the garlic and parsley. Cook for a few seconds until the mixture foams. Do not cook too long so that the garlic burns, which would make the dish bitter. Spoon the garlic butter on top of the roe and liver. Sprinkle with the lemon juice or vinegar and serve immediately.

This simple, light, 20-minute dish is made with tomatoes and wine, both pungent tastes which complement the mildness and softness of fish. We use porgy fillets here (we filleted 4 porgies and used the heads and bones to make the fish soup on page 24) but any fish can be used. The oilier fish are particularly good with this type of sauce.

¾ cup very finely chopped onions

8 small fish fillets (about 4½ ounces each)

½ cup peeled, seeded, and diced tomatoes

1½ teaspoons salt

¾ cup dry white wine

¼ cup (½ stick) butter

S E R V E S 8

⏲ 10 MINUTES

⏱ 15 TO 20 MINUTES

1 Wash the chopped onions in a sieve under cold water. Press with your hand to extrude most of the water. The washing prevents the onions from turning dark and makes them less bitter and strong-tasting.

Arrange the fillets, skin side up, in a large gratin dish and sprinkle with the onions.

2 Add the rest of the ingredients, except the butter. Place a piece of buttered waxed paper on top and bake in the center of a 400-degree oven for 10 to 12 minutes. At that point the fillets should be tender and cooked through.

Remove the fillets to a serving platter or, if you plan to serve them in the gratin dish, hold the fillets with a plate or a small lid and pour the juice into a skillet.

3 Reduce the juice to about ⅔ cup. Add the butter, piece by piece, beating with a whisk to incorporate it into the juice, and bring the mixture to a boil. As it comes to a strong boil, the mixture rises like milk ready to boil over; this is when the fat binds into the liquid.

Immediately pour the sauce over the fillets and serve.

Mackerel is an inexpensive, moist fish with few bones, so it is economical and easy to eat. Like salmon and bluefish, it has a dark layer of fatty meat under the skin, which can be removed, although some people like it. The dark, oily flesh is quite rich, so mackerel is best cooked with something acidic, such as tomato, white wine, or vinegar, rather than a cream sauce. It is excellent grilled on a barbecue or browned under the broiler to release the fat.

This is a handy recipe for a first course, picnic, late supper, or a cold buffet because it can be made ahead and kept in the refrigerator for several days.

3 large mackerel, about 1 pound each with the head, but gutted

3 cups cold water

⅓ cup white vinegar

1 teaspoon salt

3 tablespoons chopped fresh chives or parsley to decorate the top

S E R V E S 6

🕐 10 MINUTES

🕐 20 MINUTES

1 Buy the fish whole, preferably gutted. Cutting on the bias, remove the heads and cut the fish into three pieces each. Discard the heads.

In a saucepan cover the pieces of fish with the cold water, vinegar, and salt. Bring to a boil, and boil gently for 10 minutes. Remove the pieces of fish from the broth, and when they are cool enough to handle, remove the skin. You may also remove the dark meat between the skin and the white flesh (it will slide off).

2 Lift the meat from the bones, and arrange the pieces of lukewarm fish on a serving platter. Pour the sauce (recipe follows) over the top of the fish.

3 Garnish with chopped chives. Serve at room temperature or cold.

SAUCE

This sauce has the consistency of a light mayonnaise, but it's considered a vinaigrette because it's fairly thin and somewhat acidic. You can serve it with other fatty poached fish, such as herring, salmon, or bluefish; or as a dressing for meats, particularly rich ones like roast pork; salads, like coleslaw; or vegetables, such as boiled potatoes in the skin.

1 Place the egg, vinegar, mustard, salt, and pepper into the bowl of a food processor. Process and add the oil slowly. The sauce should be light—not like a mayonnaise, but rather like light cream. If it is too thick, dilute it with 1 or 2 tablespoons of water.

1 egg
3 tablespoons red wine vinegar
2 teaspoons Dijon-style mustard
1 teaspoon salt
1 teaspoon freshly ground black pepper
½ cup vegetable oil

MAYONNAISE

Be sure that the ingredients are at room temperature, especially the oil. If the oil is cold, the recipe will not work.

2 egg yolks
1 tablespoon Dijon-style mustard
1 teaspoon red wine vinegar
½ teaspoon salt
½ teaspoon pepper
2 cups oil (vegetable oil, olive oil, or a mixture of both)

1 Combine all the ingredients except the oil in a stainless-steel or glass bowl. Start adding the oil slowly, beating with a whisk. When you have used about ½ cup of oil, add it faster until all of it has been absorbed.

These proportions will make a thick mayonnaise, but this consistency is needed to hold the vegetables together. The mayonnaise may also be made in the food processor. The recipe yields 2 cups.

TIMBALES OF FISH

The word timbale refers to a mold (one small, one larger, both usually roundish in shape) and by extension to whatever is contained in the mold. Small timbales are a very handy way to use up leftovers and they're also good for serving numerous guests as they pre-portion food neatly and attractively. They can be served as a tasty first course for a dinner party or as a main luncheon course. The timbales can be molded in individual molds or in a large one. Here we are using leftover Mayonnaise of Fish.

2½ cups vegetable salad (approximately ½ the recipe on page 86)
5 ounces cooked fish flesh
½ envelope (1½ teaspoons) unflavored gelatin mixed with 2 tablespoons water
Oil to grease the mold
1 tomato cut into slices for the decoration
A few sprigs of parsley

1 Mix the vegetable salad and the pieces of fish together.
  Heat the gelatin mixture, stirring, to melt. Pour it into the
fish and vegetable salad in one stroke and mix rapidly. Work
quickly or the mixture may harden before it is combined thoroughly.

  Lightly oil 6 ¾-cup metal or porcelain molds, or a single large
one, and fill with the salad. Cover with plastic wrap and place in
the refrigerator for at least 1 to 2 hours.

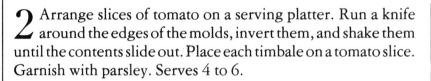

2 Arrange slices of tomato on a serving platter. Run a knife
  around the edges of the molds, invert them, and shake them
until the contents slide out. Place each timbale on a tomato slice.
Garnish with parsley. Serves 4 to 6.

PILAFF OF MUSSELS

This molded pilaff of mussels and rice is at once very good and very stately on the plate. Pilaff is wonderful when you want to stretch a small quantity of meat, fish, or shellfish. The mussels are cooked separately, then combined.

Mussels, one of the most flavorful and least expensive of shellfish, were rarely available in stores twenty years ago when I first came to the United States. However, they were plentiful all along the coasts of New York and Connecticut. Nowadays, unfortunately, most of my old musseling spots have signs reading "Polluted." Luckily, though, mussels are starting to be widely available in food stores.

Generally speaking, do not buy the very large mussels, as invariably you're just paying for shell, the mussel itself being no larger than normal. If it does turn out that the mussel is large and full, it will likely be tough. So buy heavy medium-sized mussels, approximately 15 to 18 per pound.

Just out of the water, mussels are attached to one another in bunches. They will keep in that form for at least 1½ weeks in the refrigerator; however, the meat shrinks as it loses moisture. The best mussels are the freshest. After they are separated and cleaned, they can still be kept for 3 or 4 days refrigerated.

An opened mussel is not necessarily bad. Placed in cold water or tickled inside with the point of a knife, the mussel may close, which indicates that it is still alive and good. When the

MUSSELS

4 pounds mussels

½ cup chopped onions

⅓ cup chopped celery

¼ cup chopped scallions

3 cloves garlic, peeled, crushed, and chopped (2 teaspoons)

1 tablespoon butter

1 tablespoon flour

½ cup parsley

RICE PILAFF

1 tablespoon butter

½ cup chopped onions

½ teaspoon dried thyme

1½ cups long-grain rice

3 cups water

½ teaspoon salt

SERVES 6

⏱ ⏱ 55 TO 60 MINUTES

mussel is dead, you will know by the smell.

It is necessary to wash mussels carefully to rid them of sand and mud. Left for an hour in 1 or 2 gallons of cold water with a handful of salt, they disgorge and release some of the sand. Clean the mussels by rubbing them against each other in the water. Change the water two or three times. A mussel may be full of mud and so vacuum-tight that even washing won't open it. To check for mud, push with your fingers in opposite directions to make both shells slide open. If the mussel is full of mud, discard it.

The barnacles attached to the mussels are not dirty. Actually, they impart taste to the stock. You needn't remove them unless the mussels are to be served in the shells and you feel the encrustation makes them less attractive. If the meat is removed from the shells, as it is in this pilaff, it is not necessary to remove the barnacles.

1 Separate the mussels, pull off the pieces of dry seaweed that connect them, and clean them as described above.

Place the clean mussels in a saucepan, preferably stainless steel, and cover. No additional liquid is needed—the mussels will open and release their juice. Bring to a boil, stirring once in a while as they cook. After 8 to 10 minutes they should all be open; remove from the heat.

Lift the mussels from the liquid and strain the juice through a paper towel to get rid of the sand, then pour the juice into a clean pot. We used mussels fresh out of the sea and got 2 cups of juice. The yield may be smaller if the mussels are store-bought.

2 Remove the meat from the shells. Pull out and, if you wish, discard the long, dark, string-like sinew. Most restaurants do not remove it, and it is not done when the mussels are served in the shells, but it tends to be tough, and the dish will also look more elegant.

At this stage of cooking, the mussels could be served plain with their natural juices or with the finished sauce (see next step), or served provençal as described on the opposite page.

3 To finish the sauce, add the onion, celery, scallions, and garlic to the mussel liquid, and boil gently for 10 minutes. Meanwhile, knead together the butter and flour with a whisk and, using the whisk, stir the kneaded butter directly into the broth. Add the parsley, mix well, and bring to a boil. Simmer for 2 to 3 minutes. Keep stirring with the whisk until the mixture boils so that there are no more lumps. You should have approximately 2 cups of sauce. Taste for seasoning, and add a dash of pepper if needed. Usually no salt is necessary, because the juice of the mussels is salty enough.

4 To prepare the pilaff, melt the butter in a small saucepan. Add the onions and thyme, mix well, and sauté for about 1 minute. Add the rice, and stir to coat the rice with butter. Add the water and salt, and stir until the mixture comes to a boil. Reduce the heat to very low, cover, and cook for 20 minutes.

Butter generously a ¾-cup Pyrex custard dish, and place 3 tablespoons of the cooked rice in it. Press it against the sides with a spoon to make a nest in the center. Place 6 to 8 mussels in the nest, and cover with 2 tablespoons of sauce.

5 Place another 2 tablespoons of rice on top of the mussels, press down with the back of a spoon, and invert the cup onto a serving plate. The pilaff should slide out easily. Place 3 to 4 tablespoons of sauce around the rice and a dash of parsley on top. Repeat for the other servings. Serve as soon as possible.

[The finished Pilaff of Mussels at lower right; Mussels Provençal upper right.]

MUSSELS PROVENÇAL

12 mussels, cleaned and cooked

PROVENÇAL BUTTER

¼ cup (½ stick) soft butter

1 tablespoon chopped parsley

1 clove garlic, peeled, crushed, and chopped fine

Salt and pepper to taste

⅓ cup fresh bread crumbs

1 We prepared these Mussels Provençal with some mussels we had leftover from the pilaff. They had already been cleaned and cooked. If you are starting from scratch, clean and cook the mussels following steps 1–3 on page 91. Then open the cooked mussels and place the shells containing the meat on a tray. (Discard the other shells.)

2 Combine the butter, chopped parsley, garlic, salt, and pepper. Mix well, and place a good teaspoonful of the mixture on each mussel. Sprinkle each with about 1 teaspoon of fresh bread crumbs. Heat in a 425-degree oven for 6 to 8 minutes until the butter is bubbly and the mussels are hot. Serve immediately. Six per person is a normal serving for a first course.

STEW OF CHICKEN WINGS

This is one of those international rice-based casserole dishes that can be found in most kinds of cooking around the world. The addition of saffron, shellfish, fish, and sliced sausages in the last 5 minutes of cooking would transform it into an excellent paella. Olives as well as capers are often added, but for the sake of economy we replace them with peas, zucchini, and tomatoes. If done ahead, this dish should be reheated slowly, preferably in an oven. If it is too thick, moisten with 1/2 cup of water before placing it in the oven.

Although this recipe is made with chicken wings, which are usually less expensive then whole chickens, you can also use other pieces. We use a shorter-grain rice bought in large bags which is about half the price of long-grain Carolina rice. Although converted or parboiled rice (a rice which has gone through a process to remove some of the starch) is less sticky, regular rice is good with this dish, even if it ends up a bit mushy.

Approximately 3 1/2 pounds chicken wings (18 to 20)

1 tablespoon butter

1 cup chopped onions

3/4 cup sliced scallions

1 1/2 cups rice

3 cups water

2 teaspoons salt

1/2 teaspoon freshly ground black pepper

1/2 teaspoon paprika

1/2 teaspoon turmeric

1 teaspoon oregano

3 cloves garlic, peeled and crushed (2 teaspoons)

1 cup tomatoes, seeded and cubed

3/4 cup zucchini cut into 1/4-inch dice

3/4 cup peas

1/2 cup diced green or red sweet pepper

Tabasco sauce (optional)

SERVES 6 TO 8

⏲ 10 TO 15 MINUTES

⏲ 45 TO 50 MINUTES

1 Twist the chicken wings, tucking the tip of the wing under, to make them more compact and shape them so they take less space and brown more evenly on both sides.

Heat the butter in a large pot. When it is hot and foaming, add the chicken wings, flat side down. Do not crowd the pan too much. If the chicken wings don't fit in one layer, use another skillet. Cook without disturbing on medium heat until they become very crusty and brown, then flip to the other side. The wings will release some fat, which helps the browning. Cook for about 12 to 14 minutes so they are nicely browned on all sides.

If you have used an extra skillet, combine all the pieces in the large pot. Put ½ cup water in the extra skillet to melt the solidified juice in the bottom, and add to the water to be added to the dish.

2 Add the onions and scallions to the pot and sauté for 1 minute. Add the rice and mix well so that it is coated with the fat. Add the water, salt, pepper, paprika, turmeric, oregano, and garlic and stir carefully. Bring to a boil, stirring once in a while. As soon as it boils, cover, reduce the heat to very low, and simmer for 15 minutes. Add the tomatoes, zucchini, peas, and red pepper. Cover again, and cook for another 10 minutes. Serve with or without Tabasco sauce.

RICE PANCAKE

Pan-fry leftover rice to make a good, crusty rice cake, similar to the pasta cake on page 43. Here we are making it with rice that was left over from the Stew of Chicken Wings. The bits of vegetables and meat in it make the dish particularly good. Rice holds better than pasta shells; therefore, no eggs need to be mixed in. However, a fried egg on top of the rice pancake is excellent. This rice pancake serves 3 to 4.

¼ cup vegetable oil

3 cups leftover rice, with pieces of vegetables and meat if available

Eggs to serve with the rice

1 Heat the oil in a nonstick skillet about 7 to 8 inches in diameter. Add the rice and pack by pressing it down with the back of a spoon. Cook on medium heat for 10 minutes or until nicely browned.

Flip over and cook another 5 minutes on the other side. It should be crunchy. Slide onto a plate and serve with fried eggs.

Cassoulet, a dish from the southwest of France, traditionally consists of duck or goose and roast pork or lamb, sausages, pork rind, beans and seasoning, all cooked and served in an ovenware tureen. This stew of chicken and beans is a simplified version, but nevertheless makes a very satisfying dish; flavorful, hearty, and inexpensive—ideal for a family meal.

To enhance the taste and texture of the dish, it is sprinkled with cracklings made from the skin of the chicken. A tender Boston lettuce in a cream dressing studded with more cracklings is the accompaniment.

Beans more than one or two years old need long soaking to soften them, reduce the cooking time, and restore moisture. When bought in the supermarket, the small white beans that we use in cassoulet, called navy beans or Great Northern beans, are never old enough to require soaking. If you decide to do so, however, 1 or 2 hours should be sufficient; overnight is often too long. Bubbles may show on top of the water, a sign of fermentation, which can cause digestive problems. Always start to cook beans in cold salted water. If started in hot water, they toughen and take much longer to cook.

This dish is simple to make from chicken backs and necks, left over or bought especially for this purpose. In this case we bought two whole chickens and boned them, using the flesh for the delicate chicken sauté on page 103.

4 pounds of chicken bones and parts (see Note)

1 pound white navy beans

2 large onions (approximately ¾ pound), peeled and studded with 6 cloves

3 medium to large carrots, peeled

1 rib celery

2 teaspoons salt

½ teaspoon thyme leaves

4 bay leaves

8 cups cold water

1 tomato cut in half, seeded, and coarsely chopped (¾ cup)

3 cloves garlic, peeled, crushed, and chopped (2 teaspoons)

½ cup chopped parsley

S E R V E S 6

⏱ 20 MINUTES IF YOU BONE THE CHICKEN; 10 MINUTES IF YOU BUY PARTS AND BONES

⏲ 2 TO 2½ HOURS

TO BONE A WHOLE CHICKEN

1 Cut the leg of the chicken where the skin is loose all around. Lift the leg and break it at the joint of the hip.

2 Cut through the hip joint. Hold the chicken with your knife flat and pull with the other hand to separate the leg from the rest of the carcass. Repeat with the other leg. Remove the skin from the legs, breasts, and necks (reserve for cracklings).

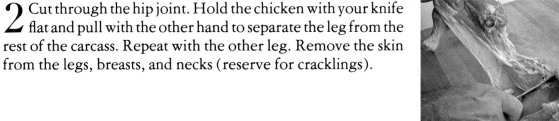

3 Remove the wings at the shoulder joint and then remove the wishbone by cutting on each side of it with a knife and pulling it out with your fingers.

4 Cut on each side of the sternum (the central breastbone).

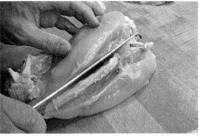

5 Cut the shoulder joint and pull out the breast on each side. You should have 2 single breasts and 2 legs with the end of the knuckles removed per chicken. Set the meat aside to make the Chicken with Mustard Sauce, or any other sautéed chicken dish.

TO PREPARE THE CASSOULET

1 Place the bones in a large kettle. Rinse the navy beans in a sieve under cold water, discarding any stones or damaged beans.

Add the beans to the bones with the onions, carrots, celery, salt, thyme, bay leaves, and 8 cups of water. Bring to a boil. Cover and boil very gently for 1½ hours. Stir every 15 or 20 minutes to prevent the beans from sticking to the bottom.

2 Pour the whole mixture into a large roasting pan. When it is cool enough, separate the bones and other vegetable solids from the beans. Put the beans back into the kettle.

3 When the bones are cool enough to handle, pick off the meat. You should have at least 2 to 2½ cups of meat. Remove the cloves from the onions, discard them, and chop the onions coarsely along with the carrots, celery, gizzards, and hearts. Add to the kettle along with the meat and mix with the beans. Add the tomato, garlic, and parsley and bring the whole dish back to a boil. Simmer for another 5 to 10 minutes.

4 Serve the cassoulet with cracklings on top. Serve the salad on the side.

NOTE: We used the gizzards, hearts, wings, and carcasses of two boned chickens (total weight approximately 1¾ pounds), plus about 1¼ pounds of chicken necks bought separately. However, any combination of backs and necks or other bones or parts can be used. Choose what's least expensive. Remove the skin and use it to make cracklings.

CRACKLINGS

Chicken skin from 2 whole chickens or the equivalent number of parts

½ teaspoon salt

1 Lay the pieces of skin flat on a large cookie sheet. Sprinkle with the salt and place in a 350-degree oven; bake without turning for 30 minutes. Turn the skin over and cook for another 15 to 20 minutes. The skins will have reduced considerably, but should be crisp and browned.

2 Let them cool off a bit. Then lift them from the fat, cut them into ½-inch pieces and set aside. The skin of two chickens should yield about 1½ cups of cracklings. Reserve the chicken fat for future use.

BOSTON LETTUCE AND CRACKLINGS

1 large or 2 small heads Boston lettuce

3 tablespoons heavy cream

1 teaspoon wine vinegar

½ teaspoon salt

¼ teaspoon freshly ground black pepper

2 teaspoons vegetable oil

½ cup chicken skin cracklings

1 Separate the leaves of the lettuce. Split the large outside leaves in the middle of the rib, and break each half leaf in half again. The smaller leaves need be cut only once. Wash carefully under cold water and drain well in a salad dryer. You should have 8 to 10 cups of loose, clean lettuce.

2 Mix the cream, vinegar, salt, and pepper well with a whisk for 10 to 15 seconds until it starts to get foamy. Add the oil; it will thicken the mixture.

Toss with the lettuce, and sprinkle with cracklings. Boston lettuce is quite tender and should not be seasoned ahead or it will wilt.

C H I C K E N   C A S S O U L E T

TUREENS OF CASSOULET

This is an alternate way of serving chicken cassoulet. The addition of sausage and bread crumbs makes it more like the authentic dish; at the same time it extends it, so that it stretches even further. We used 2½-cup tureens here, which served two people each. Use smaller onion-soup bowls if you prefer to serve one bowl per person. Figure on 1 cup of beans and 1 sausage per person, if using leftovers.

Approximately 4 cups bean mixture
2 Italian sausages, sautéed in a skillet for 4 to 5 minutes
2 knockwurst, each cut into 3 pieces
½ cup fresh bread crumbs (approximately 1 slice)
⅓ cup chicken fat (use the fat rendered from the skin if you made cracklings)

1 Add enough water to the bean mixture to make it very soupy, because the bread crumbs and the oven heat will draw out moisture. Place the mixture in individual bowls and push in large chunks of sausages or other meat. You can also use chunks of ham or pork roast as well as the type of sausages that we use in the Sausage and Potato Stew, page 109.

2 Sprinkle about 2 tablespoons of bread crumbs on top of each bowl and moisten the crumbs with chicken fat. Place in a 400-degree oven for 35 to 40 minutes, and serve piping hot directly from the oven.

This dish, which can be assembled quickly, goes well with sautéed zucchini (page 61), as well as with boiled potatoes, buttered noodles, or the rice pilaff on page 90.

You can use chicken parts or buy two chickens and bone them yourself (see page 99), reserving the bones for a stock or for the Chicken Cassoulet. Two chickens will provide you with the 8 pieces you need—4 breasts and 4 legs.

3 tablespoons butter
8 chicken breasts or legs or a combination of both, boned and skinned
1 teaspoon salt
½ teaspoon freshly ground black pepper
1 cup finely chopped onions
2 tablespoons flour
2 cups water
2 tablespoons Dijon-style mustard

S E R V E S   8

🕐 5 MINUTES IF BONED

🕐 30 TO 35 MINUTES

1 Heat the butter in a very large skillet that will accommodate the chicken without overlapping, or use two smaller skillets. Sprinkle the meat with salt and pepper. When the fat is hot, brown the pieces on medium to high heat approximately 2½ to 3 minutes on each side, until nicely browned.

Mix in the onion and keep cooking for 1 minute. Sprinkle the flour on the pieces, turning so that all the pieces are coated. Cook 1 minute to lightly brown the flour. Add the water and stir to dissolve the flour until the mixture comes to a boil. Lower the heat, cover the skillet, and boil gently for 20 minutes. Remove the meat to a serving platter.

2 Reduce the sauce to about 1½ cups and mix in the mustard. Do not allow the sauce to boil after you add the mustard. Place the chicken pieces back into the sauce and keep on very low heat for 10 to 15 minutes. This macerating of the chicken pieces in the sauce develops taste in the dish. Serve with sauce.

Bresse, the part of France where I was born, is known as the home of the best chickens in France, and many good chicken-liver recipes come from Bresse. They're used in stuffing, in pâté (page 51), or simply sautéed as we illustrate here. When shopping for chicken livers, try to get pale yellowish livers, which are fatter, sweeter, and less bitter than the dark red ones.

Livers can be easily overcooked. Generally, the technique for sautéing them, which also applies to kidneys, is to cook them very fast in extremely hot fat so that the outside gets sealed and the inside stays moist and a bit pink. Then, especially for kidneys, place them in a colander or a sieve to drain. Discard the red liquid that drains off the meat, because it tends to make the dish bitter. When the livers are served with a sauce, the sauce is made separately, then the livers or kidneys are heated in the sauce without boiling. They stay moist, tender, and mild. Of course, there are other methods of cooking livers or kidneys, such as braising, which is used for steak and kidney pie. In this case the livers are well cooked for a stronger-tasting stew.

The method that follows is a bit different from the traditional method of sautéing livers; I learned it from Danny Kaye, a great cook and friend.

NOTE: Frozen livers should be defrosted under refrigeration so that they don't lose too much moisture. Discard the liquid that collects during defrosting. Clean properly, if necessary, before using.

1¼ pounds chicken livers (see Note)

3 tablespoons vegetable oil

2 tablespoons butter

1 teaspoon salt

½ teaspoon freshly ground pepper

⅔ cup finely chopped onions

⅓ cup red wine vinegar

Approximately ⅔ cup tomato pulp (peel, seed, and chop the tomatoes into a purée; the skins and liquid can be used in stock)

1 cup chicken or beef stock

1 teaspoon softened butter

1 teaspoon flour

¼ cup finely chopped parsley

SERVES 6

🕐 12 TO 15 MINUTES

🕐 5 TO 8 MINUTES

CHICKEN LIVERS SAUTÉED WITH VINEGAR

1 The liver on the right is pale in color (our favorite), and the one on the left is darker and still has the little green bag, the gall bladder, attached to it. This bag (next to the point of the knife) should be removed, because the liquid inside (the bile) is extremely bitter. Sometimes it breaks when it is removed, and some of the liquid runs on the liver and makes it green. Any greenish part of the liver should be removed, because it will be very bitter.

2 Bring a pot of water to boil on top of the stove. Use plenty of water, and let it boil strongly. Place the livers in a sieve, and lower them into the boiling water. Stir the livers with a spoon for about 20 to 30 seconds. The water will not even have time to come to a boil again. Lift the sieve and place it on a plate so the livers can drain.

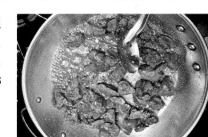

3 Heat the oil and the butter in a skillet large enough to hold all the livers without overlapping, or use two smaller skillets. When the fat is foaming hot, add the livers, salt, and pepper. Mix, and sauté on the highest heat for no more than 45 seconds to a minute.

4 Remove the livers with a slotted spoon to the sieve to drain again. Add the onions to the drippings in the skillet, and sauté for 2 to 3 minutes on medium heat until slightly browned. Add the vinegar and reduce the liquid until it becomes a glaze. Add the tomatoes and stock and bring to a boil. Make a thickening agent *(beurre manié)* by mixing the butter and the flour together with a whisk. Stir it into the sauce with the whisk. Bring to a boil, still stirring, and let boil gently for 1 minute. Taste for seasonings. Add the livers and warm gently without boiling.

Sprinkle with parsley or other fresh herbs. Serve with stewed kale (page 60) or a salad green stewed in the same manner.

This is an ideal way of using leftover roasted or poached chicken, as well as turkey the day after Thanksgiving. Use the white as well as the dark meat. It should not be assembled more than 2 hours ahead, because the lettuce will start to wilt and sink and the mayonnaise will change color on top.

The decoration can be changed and suited to your own taste. Cooked carrots, blanched scallions, tomato, hard-boiled eggs, and olives can be used to create different effects.

Leftover chicken (1 leg and 1 breast)
4 to 5 slices carrots (made with a vegetable peeler)
2 or 3 pieces of the green of scallion
1 hard-cooked egg
6 cups shredded lettuce (iceberg or Boston)
1 cup mayonnaise (see page 88)
1 ripe tomato
2 or 3 basil leaves or parsley to decorate the center

S E R V E S   4   T O   6

⏱ 1 5   M I N U T E S

1 Bone the chicken and cut it into slices. If some of the meat, especially the dark meat, is too bulky, press it down to flatten so that it is as flat as the rest of the slices.

Drop the slices of carrot into boiling water, bring back to a boil, and boil for about 1½ minutes. Cool under cold water and pat dry. Blanch the scallion for 15 to 20 seconds in the boiling water to wilt, and cool under cold water. Hard-cook the egg (page 36). Cool and remove the shell.

2 Separate the lettuce leaves, wash and dry. Pile the leaves together, roll, and cut into julienne pieces. Mound the lettuce in the center of a nice glass or crystal bowl. It should be domed, not flat. Arrange the slices of chicken all over the lettuce to cover it. Work gently with your fingers to keep the shape of the salad.

3 With a small spatula, spread the mayonnaise on top of the chicken. Work gently to keep the shape of the dish. Smooth the surface with the spatula.

4 Arrange 4 slices of carrot crisscrossing on the mayonnaise to imitate a ribbon on a package. To make the carrot stand out more, outline each slice with thin strips of scallion.

5 Cut the tomato into wedges and arrange around the edges. Slice the egg, and arrange the slices in each of the four sections of the dish. Make a hole through the carrot in the middle, and insert the basil leaves. Serve immediately, or cover lightly with plastic wrap and refrigerate until serving time.

This is another one of those dishes that evoke happy memories. My mother used to make it all the time when I was growing up and she still does, especially when my brothers and I visit. In Lyons, where I come from, we use a large uncooked sausage, a type of *cotechino* or Savoy sausage called a *cervelas.* Unless you make your own sausage, the dish can be duplicated with Italian sausage, either the sweet or the hot or both. Large knockwurst, bratwurst, or even frankfurters or kielbasa can also be used. In this recipe we mix uncooked and cooked sausages. If you use uncooked sausages, such as Italian, the fat that is released as they brown will help brown the potatoes and onions. If you use only cooked sausages, such as knockwurst, kielbasa, or frankfurters, add some oil when browning them so that there is enough fat in the pan to brown the potatoes and the onions. Keep in mind that the sausages, depending on the type, will impart their flavor, whether spicy, anise, or smoky, to the onions and the potatoes. A strong, tough salad, such as escarole with a garlic mustard dressing, is particularly well suited to serve with this dish.

1 pound Italian sausages (a mixture of hot and sweet)

1 pound knockwurst (6 sausages)

3 bratwurst (½ pound of sausages made of veal and pork)

6 medium onions, peeled (1 pound)

2 pounds small to medium potatoes, peeled (approximately 15)

6–8 cloves garlic, unpeeled

S E R V E S   6

🕙 15   M I N U T E S

🕙 1   H O U R

1 Here are different types of sausage: In the back, knockwurst on the left and bratwurst on the right; in the front, hot and sweet Italian sausages.

2 Place the uncooked (Italian) sausages and ⅓ cup water in a large pot so that they are in one layer. Cook slowly on medium heat. The water will evaporate after a few minutes but will help the sausages to release their fat. After 5 minutes, add the knockwurst and the bratwurst to brown. After 10 to 12 minutes, the sausages should be brown all over. Remove to a plate and set aside.

If you are using only the knockwurst, bratwurst, and/or kielbasa, add ⅓ cup oil to the pan and omit the water. Add the onions and potatoes to the fat and brown on medium to low heat, uncovered, for approximately 20 minutes. Add the garlic and sausages and cook another 20 minutes, covered, on very low heat. Taste for seasoning and add salt if needed.

3 Serve the potatoes and sausages with a little bit of the natural juices and a tough, chewy, and slightly bitter salad green, like escarole (recipe follows).

ESCAROLE SALAD WITH GARLIC DRESSING

1 large head or two small heads escarole
2 teaspoons Dijon-style mustard
2 cloves garlic, peeled, crushed, and chopped very fine (1 teaspoon)
2 teaspoons wine vinegar
¼ teaspoon freshly ground black pepper
¼ teaspoon salt
⅓ cup vegetable oil

1 If the ribs of the escarole, especially on the outside leaves, are too wide, split in half through the center and cut into 2-inch pieces. Wash thoroughly and drain well in a salad dryer; there should be no extra water left in the salad. You should have approximately 8 to 9 cups of washed and diced escarole.

2 Mix together all the dressing ingredients except the oil. Add the oil slowly, mixing with a whisk or a spoon. Do not try to blend the mixture well. It is all right if it is separated. Five minutes before serving, toss the salad with the vinaigrette.

Breast of lamb is inexpensive and available in most supermarkets. The cut may vary slightly, depending on where you buy it. Sometimes it doesn't include the fleshy narrow side but only the length of the ribs. Sometimes the large cartilages and bones have been removed from the ends of the ribs, and sometimes not, in which case you have to cut through the bone as you cut between the ribs.

I prefer to use a breast with the bones in. Lamb breast is very tricky to bone, and the holes throughout the meat cause problems if the meat is stuffed. Moreover, the bones hold the breast in shape during cooking and add a lot of flavor. When the lamb is cooked, the bones can be removed easily just by twisting. In fact, their looseness is an indication of doneness.

This cut of lamb should always be cooked well done. It consists of layers of meat and fat, so if the meat is rare, the fat and sinew between meat layers are left uncooked. Only solid pieces of meat without these layers, like rack of lamb, can be cooked rare.

Lamb breast lends itself very well to stuffing; the first of the three following recipes is for such a dish. The next two show how to use the breast to make a good lamb stew and a Lamb Provençal, in which the breast is roasted in the oven.

The breast is very good stuffed. First, it's a flat piece of meat on top of bone, and there's a certain logic to stuffing between the meat and the bone. In addition, the stuffing extends the dish, making it go further, as there's not much meat on the bones. Lamb breast in particular has a rich, strong taste, and the meat is moist and fatty; it "nourishes" the stuffing—the stuffing absorbs the good taste of the meat. When you stuff a dry meat, such as veal or chicken, the principle works in reverse: you need a rich stuffing, such as one of pork, so that the stuffing "nourishes" the meat.

Because there are several layers in the breast, it is tricky to find the right pocket for the stuffing. I just slice directly on top of the bone, lift up the whole layer, and stuff that cavity.

Almost any stuffing can be used—all bread or vegetables or meat, as well as a mixture. The recipe given here uses the trimmings of the lamb itself, which hold the stuffing together.

The stuffing or even the whole dish can be made ahead and reheated.

2 lamb breasts, about 1½ pounds each

4 ounces stale bread

1 cup milk

1 teaspoon butter

½ cup diced onions

3 cloves garlic, peeled, crushed, and chopped (1½ teaspoons)

¼ cup chopped parsley

½ teaspoon thyme leaves

½ teaspoon dry sage

½ teaspoon salt

½ teaspoon freshly ground black pepper

VEGETABLE GARNISH

⅓ cup water

3 cups carrot sticks, 1½ inches long

3 cups peeled, quartered onions, separated into layers

1 Trim the reddish layer of skin (the fell or pelt) from both breasts if it is tough. (The fell is tender in young animals and doesn't have to be removed.) Cut off the boneless end to use in the stuffing. You should be able to get approximately 4 to 5 ounces of meat from each breast. Cut the ends into smaller pieces, then purée in the food processor.

2 Insert your knife on top of the bone and cut as far as you can on all sides, without opening the edges, to make a pouch. Keep the blade flat. Note that only one side of the breast should be opened.

3 Mash the bread and milk into a soft mixture. If the bread is very dry, you may need more milk.
   Melt the butter in a skillet. Add the onions and sauté gently for about 2 minutes. Stir in the garlic. Turn the onions and garlic into a bowl with the parsley, thyme, sage, salt, pepper, bread, and raw puréed meat. Divide the stuffing equally between both breasts.

4 Tie the roast at one end with a single knot, not too tightly. Be sure to use fairly thick cotton kitchen twine so it doesn't cut your finger or go through the meat. Make a loop with the twine.

5 Slide the loop underneath.

6 Pull up to make one knot. Repeat every 1½ to 2 inches.

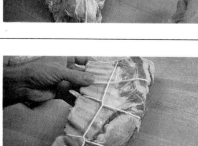

7 When you come to the end, turn the roast upside down. Bring the twine around and twist it around each string across. Finally, come around and tie the end of the string to the first knot. (If you find it easier, you may tie the roast with individual knots spaced 1 inch apart.)

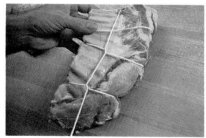

8 Sprinkle the breasts with additional salt and pepper and place them fleshy or fatty side down in a skillet large enough to accommodate them without overlapping. There's no need to add fat, as there's still a small layer of fat on the meat. Brown for 6 to 7 minutes on medium high heat. Turn and brown 6 to 7 minutes more. Cover the pan with a lid, reduce the heat to low, and let cook gently for 20 minutes.

9 Pour out the fat that has accumulated around the meat, and add ⅓ cup of water, the carrots, and the onions. Cover and braise gently on low heat for 1 hour.

10 Place the meat on a cutting board and remove the twine. Pull off the ribs by cutting along each rib and twisting the bone off. If the meat is cooked, the bone will slide out easily.

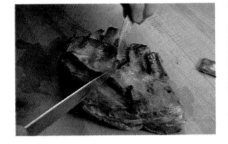

11 Slice into 1½-inch slices, and arrange on a platter or on individual plates with the vegetables and the natural gravy. Serve immediately.

Breast of lamb, because it is rich, tasty, inexpensive, and very moist, is particularly suitable for this lamb stew. Navarin of Lamb is a standard in the spring when the new vegetables come into season. The stew can be made ahead and reheated, or even frozen, which makes it ideal for a large family. Notice that the meat is browned without any added fat. After a few minutes of cooking, enough fat is released from the meat to brown it. The fat is later discarded. This makes a flavorful stew, not too fatty, easy to digest, and not too high in calories.

1¾ pounds of lamb (2 breasts cut into about 10 pieces)

1 cup sliced onions

1 tablespoon flour

3 to 4 cloves garlic, peeled and crushed (1½ teaspoons)

3 cups water

2 teaspoons salt

½ teaspoon pepper

2 bay leaves

About 5 potatoes (1 pound), peeled and cubed into 1½-inch dice

5 carrots (approximately 2 cups), cut into sticks

1 cup frozen baby peas (½ a 12-ounce package)

S E R V E S   6

⏱ 1 0   M I N U T E S

⏱ 1 ½   H O U R S

1 Remove the pelt from the lamb and trim the fat from the top. (See the technique for Stuffed Breast of Lamb.) When the meat is mostly defatted, cut it into strips through the ribs. Place the meat, fat side down, in a pot large enough so that the pieces do not overlap. (If need be, use a pot and an extra skillet so that the meat is not too crowded.) Cook on low to medium heat for about 15 minutes, turning the pieces until they are browned all over. If you have used an extra skillet, combine the meat in the large pot.

2 Place a lid on top of the pot. Hold the lid with one hand and the pot by the handle with the other, and invert them over the sink to pour out the fat released from the meat. If you have used an extra skillet, deglaze it with a little bit of water to release the solidified juices, and set it aside.

Add the onions to the meat and sauté for 1 minute on medium heat. Add the flour, mix well, and cook again for 1 minute. Then add the garlic, water, the deglazed juices, if any, from the extra skillet, salt, pepper, and bay leaves. Bring to a boil, cover, and boil gently for 30 minutes. Add the potatoes and carrots, and boil gently for another 25 minutes. Finally, add the peas and cook for 5 more minutes.

3 Arrange the meat and vegetables on a large platter or individual plates. This stew doesn't have much sauce. The vegetables should be cooked and soft, and the potatoes a bit mushy. Serve very hot.

Lamb Provençal is another way of using breast of lamb. The breasts are left whole and poached in water to make the meat tender and to melt most of the fat from inside the layers. The lamb is then browned in the oven, topped with a mixture of parsley, garlic, onion, and bread crumbs, and baked some more. After poaching, the breasts could be grilled on a barbecue or crisped under the broiler. They will be crusty on top, but cooked inside.

Whole onions baked in aluminum foil, a very simple recipe, go well with this dish.

2 breasts of lamb, approximately 1½ to 1¾ pounds

½ teaspoon salt

½ teaspoon freshly ground black pepper

1 cup fresh bread crumbs (about 1½ slices fresh bread chopped in the food processor)

½ cup chopped parsley leaves

2 cloves garlic, peeled, crushed, and chopped fine

2 tablespoons vegetable oil

S E R V E S   4

⏱ 1 0   M I N U T E S

🍲 2   H O U R S

1 Place the breasts of lamb in a large pot, cover them with cold water, and bring to a boil. Skim off any scum that rises to the top. Lower the heat, cover, and boil very gently for 1 hour. Remove the meat and allow it to cool slightly. (Save the stock; it can be used to make Scotch barley soup.) Sprinkle the meat with salt and pepper, and place it in a roasting pan in a 375-degree oven for 30 minutes.

Make fresh bread crumbs in a food processor and combine with the chopped parsley, garlic and oil. The mixture should be moist.

Remove the breasts from the oven and cover the tops with the bread mixture. Pat gently with your hand to hold the crumbs in place as you spread them. Return the lamb to the oven for 30 minutes. It should be nicely browned and well done.

2 To serve, cut the breasts apart between the ribs and arrange each rib on a plate with a baked onion (recipe follows). Notice that the tips of the bones on the lamb breasts stick out, indicating that the meat has shrunk away from the bones and is fully cooked.

ONIONS IN PAPILLOTE

1 Place each onion on a piece of aluminum foil and top it with a teaspoon of vegetable oil and a dash of salt.

2 Enclose the onions and bake them in a 375-degree oven for 45 to 50 minutes. The onions should be soft and cooked throughout but not falling apart. Allow 1 onion per person.

6 whole onions, about 4 ounces each, peeled

2 tablespoons vegetable oil

Salt

6 pieces of 6-inch-square aluminum

This stewed potato dish was one of my father's favorites. It recalls summer for me when the garden gave forth those tiny waxy potatoes we call *quenelles* in Lyons, and which are particularly good in this dish. This is true family food and it remains a favorite in both my mother's home and ours.

Potato Ragoût is usually made with lardons (short strips of salt pork) but it can also be made with leftover ham or sausage. Salt pork (also called cured salt pork, sweet pickle, or corned belly, depending on what part of the country you're in) comes from the same piece of belly as bacon. The difference is that though it's salted like bacon, it is not smoked. Many recipes direct you to blanch salt pork to make it less salty. In this recipe, you need only wash it well under cold water.

Potato Ragoût reheats well and is excellent served with a tough, slightly bitter green, such as curly endive or escarole, seasoned with a strong vinegary or garlicky dressing.

1 10-ounce slab salt pork

3 large onions, peeled and quartered (1 pound)

2 tablespoons flour

4 cloves garlic, peeled, crushed, and coarsely chopped (2 teaspoons)

3 bay leaves

1 branch fresh thyme, or ½ teaspoon dried thyme leaves

2½ cups water

2½ pounds tiny potatoes, peeled, or the same amount of large potatoes, peeled and cut into chunks

S E R V E S   6

⏱ 20 TO 25 MINUTES

🕐 1 HOUR

1 Rinse the slab of salt pork under running water, then cut it into ½-inch strips. Pile the strips together and cut into the ¼- to ½-inch strips that we call lardons. Don't remove the rind as it gives the sauce a slightly gelatinous texture and is quite good to eat.

The candied peels of oranges and other citrus fruits—grapefruit, limes, and lemons—are delicious all by themselves, but are also very useful in pastries and innumerable other desserts. They keep for months in a jar in the refrigerator, to be cut into a julienne and used to decorate a cold or hot orange soufflé or poached fruit. Used to top butter cream on a cake, they are very elegant and flavorful. Packed into little jars, candied peels make an attractive and appealing gift for friends.

Use the peels from the grapefruit or oranges that you squeeze for breakfast juice; do the same when you use freshly squeezed lemon juice. Peels can be accumulated over several days and kept in a plastic bag in the refrigerator.

Often the peel of fruit is removed with a vegetable peeler and only the thin part of the skin is candied. We candied the whole peel—the top surface, which has most of the taste, as well as the cottony part underneath. The skins are blanched several times in water and rinsed to remove some of the bitterness. The slight bitterness that they retain is desirable.

We offer two variations: chocolate-dipped peels, and candied rinds mixed with dried fruit and macerated in spirits.

3 large oranges with thick, shiny skin

1 grapefruit, preferably pink

2 large limes

2 lemons

1 ½ cups sugar, plus extra sugar to roll the peels in

YIELD: 4 DOZEN PIECES

🕐 15 MINUTES

🕐 1 ½ HOURS

1 With a knife, make incisions through the skin of each piece of fruit to separate it into six sections. Separate the skin from the fruit.

2 Place the peels in a pot and cover with cold water. Use enough water so that the peels are well covered. Bring to a strong boil and let boil for about 30 seconds. Pour into a colander, rinse under cold water, and rinse the pot. Return the peels to the pot, add water, cover, and repeat. Return the peels to the clean pot again and add 8 cups of water and the sugar. Bring to a boil and boil gently, uncovered, for about 1 ½ hours. The skins should be almost transparent, and there should be just enough thick syrup to coat them.

3 Transfer the peels to a cookie sheet covered with sugar.

4 Roll them in the sugar, arrange them on another cookie sheet, and let them cool, dry, and harden for at least 1 hour. Strain the sugar and return it to the sugar bin. (Save any lumps to mix with the sugar for poached oranges, page 135.)

CANDIED PEELS IN CHOCOLATE

Chocolate-dipped candied peels make a very elegant, delicious ending to a meal. Serve them with after-dinner brandy or liqueur. Or use them to decorate a cake, or chopped to flavor pastry cream for crêpes or a cake.

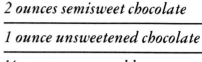

2 ounces semisweet chocolate

1 ounce unsweetened chocolate

½ teaspoon vegetable or peanut oil

12 candied orange peels

1 Melt both kinds of chocolate in the top of a double boiler and stir in the oil. Do not let the chocolate get too hot or it will lose much of its shininess.

Pour the melted chocolate into a narrow dish or glass. Dip approximately half an orange peel in the chocolate, lift it, and let the excess chocolate drip off for a few seconds.

2 Place the peel on an oiled tray. Repeat for all the rinds. Let them set in the refrigerator for at least 30 minutes. Lift the pieces from the oiled tray (some of the chocolate will stay on the tray) and arrange them on a platter, or place them in a jar for storage in the refrigerator.

MACERATED CANDIED FRUITS

These diced candied fruits are of higher quality than store-bought ones, are without coloring and preservatives, and are very inexpensive. The mixture is ideal for fruitcakes, soufflés, or charlottes, or as a flavoring for pastry cream.

½ cup dried apricots

1 ½ cups mixture of different candied peels

½ cup dark raisins

½ cup Cognac, Scotch, rum, or orange liqueur

1 Cut the apricot halves and the candied peels into ¼-inch dice and combine them with the raisins and liquor. Pour into a small jar, cover tightly, and place in the refrigerator. The mixture will keep for months.

2 Clockwise from top: Poached Oranges; Candied Citrus Peels; a poached orange topped with slivered candied peel; Candied Peels in Chocolate; plain Candied Citrus Peels; and a jar of Macerated Candied Fruits.

P O A C H E D   O R A N G E S

When people think of poached fruits, pears usually come to mind, or dried fruits such as apricots or prunes. However, oranges are excellent poached. The poaching seems to concentrate the orange flavor and the syrup keeps the oranges looking fresh and glossy. Plus poached oranges don't leak or get limp on the plate the way fresh oranges do. We poach whole oranges here, though slices can also be poached, in which case you should reduce the cooking time to 1 minute.

6 large seedless oranges

⅓ cup sugar

1 or 2 tablespoons Grand Marnier or homemade orange liqueur (see page 170)

⅓ cup water

S E R V E S   6

⏱ 10 TO 15 MINUTES

⏱ 5 TO 10 MINUTES

1 Peel the oranges with a sharp knife, preferably stainless steel. Be sure to cut through the first and second layers of the skin so that the orange is completely peeled.

2 Place the oranges in a saucepan with the sugar and ⅓ cup of water. Cover, bring to a boil, and simmer gently for 5 minutes. Remove the oranges to a bowl or serving dish.

Cook the syrup down to approximately ⅓ cup, and pour the syrup over the oranges. When cool or at serving time, sprinkle the oranges with 1 or 2 tablespoons of orange liqueur. Serve plain or with slivered candied peels on top or with a slice of pound cake.

This simple dessert can be made several days ahead; it improves when left to macerate in the refrigerator for a few days. Although it's a great favorite in our house, its bittersweet taste may not please every palate. Pick firm, thick-skinned citrus fruits—grapefruit, oranges, lemons, and limes. Unless you can find seedless varieties, be sure to remove the seeds, which impart bitterness when cooked.

This compote is superior served ice cold with a slice of pound cake or brioche, with rice or vanilla pudding, as well as with ice cream. It can also be used between layers of cake if you reduce the syrup completely until the fruits are just moist, so that it doesn't run down the cake. Let it cool, and when it is cold and thick, spread it on the cake. It can be mixed into a charlotte or a Bavarian, or in cake batter instead of diced candied fruits. Finally, it makes a great filling for crêpes. It is akin to the candied fruit mixture and candied peels described on pages 134 and 131. Slice the fruit thin, whether by hand or in a food processor.

½ medium-size grapefruit, cut into ¼-inch slices, seeds removed (about 1 cup)

2 medium-size oranges, cut in half, sliced into ¼-inch slices, seeds removed (about 2 ½ cups)

1 large lime, cut in half, sliced into ¼-inch slices, seeds removed (about ¾ cup)

¾ cup sugar

½ cup dark raisins

1 tablespoon dark rum, Cognac, or other spirits

S E R V E S   6

⏱ 10 MINUTES

🍲 1 ¹/₂ HOURS

1 Slice all the fruit and remove any seeds. Place the fruit in a saucepan, preferably stainless steel, and cover generously with water. Bring to a boil, and let boil for about 10 to 15 seconds. (The blanching of the fruit eliminates some of its bitterness.)

Pour into a colander, discarding the liquid, and rinse the fruit under cold water. Return the fruit to the saucepan with 4 cups of water and the sugar. Bring to a boil. Boil gently, uncovered, for 50 minutes. Skim off any scum that comes to the surface, especially during the first half hour of cooking. After 50 minutes, add the raisins and continue to cook for another 10 minutes. There should be just enough liquid left to baste and wet the fruit. Let cool to room temperature, cover, and refrigerate until ready to use.

2 When cool, add 1 tablespoon of rum, Cognac, or other alcohol to the mixture (optional) and serve in small, deep dishes decorated with a sprig of mint.

These sugar-coated fruits are not at all like the candied apples of our youth, because the sugar isn't cooked around the fruit and it doesn't get hard in that inimitable teeth-destroying way. This sugar coating firms up around the fruit, but it's basically more crumbly, much more delicate, and somewhat easier to eat.

Different kinds of fruit can be used so long as they are dry, so that the sugar coating doesn't get soggy and fall off. Uncut whole fruits are the best, from cherries to strawberries to blueberries. Grapes are ideal, and orange (or, better, tangerine) sections work well, providing that you don't break the membranes when you segment them and let the juice escape. With the right fruits, the sugar crystallizes and hardens around the fruit in less than 1 hour. When the crystallized layer is hard, the fruit will keep for several days in a cool, dry place. An excellent variation is to freeze the crystallized fruits. The hard sugar coating around the frozen fruit makes them resemble sherbet or frozen fruit jellies.

3 cups seedless grapes (see Note)

2 oranges or tangerines, peeled and separated into sections (Be sure not to break the membranes; the sections should be dry.)

1 egg white, beaten lightly with a fork

2 cups sugar

SERVES 6 TO 8

⏱ 15 MINUTES

NOTE: For this recipe, we used 1 cup each of Thompson grapes (a seedless, white oblong grape), dark flame seedless grapes (a pink sweet grape), and black exotic grapes (a large, fleshy, and round black grape).

1 Dip the fruit into the egg white, which should be only slightly frothy.

2 Lift up the fruit, using a fork or your fingers. Don't take too much egg white; the fruit should be just barely wet. (The egg white could also be brushed on the fruit with a pastry brush.)

Place about 10 to 12 pieces of fruit in a cake pan or on a cookie sheet with the sugar, and shake the pan so that the fruit rolls around and gets coated with the sugar.

3 Place the pieces on a cookie sheet and let them dry, either outside or inside the refrigerator. Serve with a sprig of mint for decoration. Sieve the used sugar to rid it of lumps and return it to the sugar canister.

Apple fritters, sprinkled with confectioners' sugar and eaten piping hot, make an utterly delicious dessert. They are simplicity itself; they are easy to make, and the ingredients are inexpensive and always available. I've used Granny Smith apples, a tart kind of apple that holds its shape well, as would Red or Golden Delicious or Pippin. Actually, you could use more acidic apples that break down a little faster, like the McIntosh, Rome Beauty, Macoun, and Jonathan. Sprinkle them with a little more sugar before serving to counter the acidity, and reduce the cooking time slightly.

When you make fritters, whether with fruit or vegetables, you can choose from a variety of shapes and two different methods. The fruit or vegetable can simply be cut into sticks or slices or fan shapes and dipped into the batter and fried, or it can be chopped coarsely or cut into a julienne and mixed *into* the batter and fried like a pancake. You have a choice of batters as well. I demonstrate two different ones here. One is a beer batter that can be put together extremely fast and makes a fritter that's fairly crisp on the outside and soft and yeasty on the inside. The other is an egg batter, which makes fritters that are spongy and soufflélike in texture—soft and creamy outside and in. There's a third batter on page 57 which you can also use for apples. Each of these batters has its own distinct texture and bite; the one you decide to use is a question of personal taste.

THE OIL: Cottonseed, sunflower, and grapeseed oil are particularly good oils for frying because they withstand high temperatures without breaking down. (An oil that's broken down becomes foamy and develops an acrid and bitter smell.) Use enough oil, between 2 and 3 inches, so that the fritters float freely.

THE BATTER: When you make any batter (this includes batters for crêpes and pancakes and the like), don't add all the liquid to the flour at once. You want to start with a thick batter because it's easier to whisk out lumps when they're embedded in a thickish mass rather than floating on top of a thin liquid. The remaining liquid can be added once the batter is smooth like silk.

TEMPERATURE: You'll find, as you get accustomed to frying in batter, that some batters brown faster than others and have to cook at a lower temperature. Of the two that follow, the egg batter should be cooked at a slightly lower temperature because the beaten egg white and milk brown very fast.

BEER BATTER

1 can (12 ounces) beer

1½ cups flour

*2 pounds apples
    (approximately 6 to 8)*

Oil for deep frying

1 Pour about ⅔ of the beer into the flour and beat with a whisk until smooth. Then beat in the rest of the beer. The batter should have the consistency of a thick, heavy syrup. Although it can be used right away, the batter improves if left at room temperature for about an hour; it ferments slightly, which brings out the yeasty taste and makes the fritter puff more when fried.

2 Peel and core the apples. Cut them into slices ¼ to ⅜ inch thick. Stack the slices on top of one another and cut them into sticks about ¼ inch wide (a very coarse julienne).

Mix the apple sticks into the batter. Heat the oil to about 350 degrees, and gently slide about 2 to 3 tablespoons of the mixture into the hot oil. Cook only a few fritters at a time; the size of your frying pan will determine how many. Cook approximately 1½ minutes on each side.

3 Lift the fritters out with a slotted spoon and drain on paper towels. Then sprinkle with confectioners' sugar.

EGG BATTER

1 cup flour
2 eggs, separated
1 tablespoon sugar
½ teaspoon salt
¾ cup milk
2 pounds apples
Oil for deep frying
Confectioners' sugar

1 Mix the flour, egg yolks, sugar, salt, and ½ cup milk together. Beat with a whisk until smooth and thick. Mix in the rest of the milk.

Beat the 2 egg whites by hand or by machine in a clean, un-lined copper bowl or a stainless-steel bowl (see Beating Egg Whites, page 49).

2 When the whites are firm but not dry (they shouldn't be grainy, weepy, or full of little holes, which would indicate overbeating), fold them into the batter with a rubber spatula. Fold from the center of the bowl and come up the sides, trying to lift the mixture with each stroke. Notice that the batter is thick, shiny, and smooth. It can be kept 1 or 2 days in the refrigerator or used right away.

3 Peel the apples with a small knife or a vegetable peeler. Core and slice them into ¼-to-⅜-inch-thick rings (or stack the slices and sliver them into sticks. If you do not have a corer, peel and slice the apples, then cut out the center seeds with a knife.

4 Place four or five rings in the batter. Heat 2 or 3 inches of oil in a skillet or flat-bottomed wok to about 330 degrees. Lift each ring from the batter and slide it gently into the hot oil, taking care not to splatter the oil. Cook 2½ minutes on each side. Flip the rings with a slotted spoon. When done, remove and place them on a cookie sheet lined with paper toweling. Sprinkle with confectioners' sugar and serve immediately.

This recipe serves 8.

This dessert is universal in home cooking, as well as in country inns and expensive restaurants. Only a few ingredients are used, and the dish is inexpensive, quickly prepared, and can be made the year round. It is best to use an apple that will keep its shape during cooking, such as Golden or Red Delicious, Russet, Granny Smith, or Pippin.

The apples look best when they have just come out of the oven; they are puffed from the heat and look glossy and rich. Serve them barely lukewarm, however, even though they will shrivel a bit as they cool. The apples, basted with the juice, can be reheated the day after, or make them into one of the variations that follow.

The mixture of apricot jam, maple syrup, and butter makes a very good flavorful sauce. If you don't have maple syrup, you can substitute granulated sugar. You could also add lemon juice, cinnamon, mace, nutmeg, or any other spice that you like.

6 large apples (2 pounds)

⅓ cup apricot jam

⅓ cup light maple syrup

3 tablespoons butter, cut into 6 pieces

S E R V E S   6

⏱ 10 TO 15 MINUTES

🕐 1   HOUR

1 Using a knife, cut through the center of each apple to remove the seeds, or use a corer. Be careful to plunge the corer straight down so that it doesn't veer off center and miss the core. If this happens, use the knife or corer to remove any remaining seeds from the center. You should have a clean, round opening at each end.

2 With the point of a knife make an incision in the skin about a third of the way down the apple. Cut through the skin approximately ⅛ to ¼ of an inch deep. As the apple cooks, the flesh expands and the apple above this cut will lift up like a lid. Without this scoring, the apple would burst.

3 Arrange the apples in a gratin dish or other ovenproof dish that is attractive enough to be brought to the table. We used a round glass dish. Coat the apples with the apricot jam and maple syrup, and dot with the pieces of butter. Bake in a 375-degree oven for 30 minutes, baste with the juice, and cook another 25 to 30 minutes.

The cooked apples should be cooked throughout—plump, brown, and soft to the touch. They are delicious served with a slice of pound cake or with cold sour cream.

A P P L E   M E R I N G U E

Whether you use leftover baked apples from the Apple Bonne Femme, or apples cooked especially for this dish, the Apple Meringue makes an interesting dessert. If you cook the apples especially for this dish, omit the apricot jam; you really don't need that extra sweetness with the meringue. The apples can be cooked days ahead, but the addition of the meringue and the browning should be done as close as possible to serving time. The apples can be cooked ahead, covered with meringue and baked, in which case they will be cool on the inside and hot on the outside. The dish could also be prepared with hot or lukewarm apples, or cold apples that have been reheated—it's a matter of personal taste. Serve with the sauce left from the Apple Bonne Femme, or the cooking juices if you bake the apples especially for this recipe.

A meringue is nothing more than beaten egg whites with the addition of sugar. The standard proportions for meringue are 1 cup sugar to 4 egg whites. (We used a little less sugar in this meringue because the apples have already been sweetened.) The sugar stabilizes the beaten egg whites, preventing them from breaking down; it makes them shiny and elastic.

Meringue can be piped out on trays and dried in the oven, then stored in a tin to be served with ice cream, whipped cream, or fresh fruit, or spread on top of pies, such as lemon meringue pie, or used to make buttercreams and mousses.

2 egg whites

⅓ cup sugar

3 whole baked apples (can be left over from Apple Bonne Femme)

S E R V E S   3

🕐 10 MINUTES IF YOU USE COOKED APPLES

🕐 5 MINUTES

1 Beat the egg whites by hand or machine. (See the instructions for beating egg whites in the Lettuce Soufflé recipe on page 49.) When they are firm and hold a peak, add the sugar and keep beating for about 15 to 20 seconds, until the whites are smooth, shiny, and firm.

2 Arrange the apples on a large ovenproof platter or on individual plates that can go in the oven.

Fit a pastry bag with a ½-inch star tube and fill it with the meringue. Pipe the meringue onto the apples, either in a spiral around the apple (right), or in strips from bottom to top (left), one next to the other. Cover the apples completely, finishing with a little crown on top.

3 Heat the meringue apples in a 450-degree oven for 5 minutes. Serve immediately with the sauce from the cooking of the apples.

This variation using leftover Apple Bonne Femme is very easy to make. It is ideal for a party because it can be prepared ahead and reheated just before serving. It is superb served lukewarm with cold sour cream or unsweetened whipped cream. I developed the recipe at the restaurant La Potagerie, where we made it fresh every day for between 1,200 and 1,400 people. We made it with day-old brioches, which we sliced and combined with raisins, melted butter, cinnamon, sliced fresh apple, and applesauce, then baked in the oven. We served it warm with whipped cream or hard sauce.

3 baked apples with juice (can be left over from Apple Bonne Femme)

4 slices white bread

½ cup dark raisins

2 ounces (½ stick) soft butter

1 teaspoon cinnamon

S E R V E S 6

🕙 10 MINUTES IF YOU USE COOKED APPLES

🕐 30 TO 35 MINUTES

1 Cut the apples into pieces and crush them, peel and all, directly in the pan in which you baked the apples in order to absorb all the good sauce. Break the bread into pieces and add it to the pan with the raisins, the butter, and the cinnamon. Mash well with a fork. The mixture should be soft and mushy.

2 Smooth the top with a fork and bake in a 400-degree oven for 30 to 35 minutes, until browned and crusty on top. Spoon onto individual plates, or use an ice-cream scoop if you want nice rounded servings. Serve lukewarm with fresh whipped cream or sour cream.

A P P L E G A L E T T E

A galette is almost the same as a tart, except that a tart is made in a flan ring or quiche pan, whereas a galette is free form. The tart also tends to be thicker than the galette, which is thin, large, and crusty, like a pizza. A galette is ideal for dinner parties, because it can be cooked ahead, and it keeps well, looks good, tastes good, and is easy to eat. It should be eaten at room temperature, not cold.

Apples and pears work well in galettes. Fruits that give off a great deal of liquid, such as rhubarb, plums, and cherries, can be used but require an adjustment. To compensate for the liquid, mix a few tablespoons of flour and sugar and spread the mixture on top of the dough before arranging the fruit. During cooking the mixture will absorb the juice and keep it from spilling all over the oven.

The most common mistakes in making the galette are using too much apple and making the dough too thick. The dough, *pâte brisée,* should not be more than 1/8 inch thick, and a few apples spread out or fanned on top in one layer are sufficient. Do not remove the galette from the oven too soon; it should be very well cooked, from 65 to 75 minutes at 400 degrees. It should be very crusty, thin, and soft inside. Do not worry about the discoloration of the apples after you peel and arrange them on the dough. The discoloration will not be apparent after cooking.

½ recipe pâte brisée *(page 152)*

5 large apples

¼ cup sugar

3 tablespoons butter, cut into small pieces

4 tablespoons apricot preserves

1 tablespoon Calvados or Cognac (optional)

S E R V E S 8 T O 1 2

⏱ 3 0 M I N U T E S

🕐 6 5 T O 7 5 M I N U T E S

1 Make *pâte brisée.* Roll out the dough ⅛ to ¹⁄₁₆ inch thick, in a shape that fits roughly on a cookie sheet—approximately 16 × 14 inches. (The best cookie sheets are made of heavy aluminum that is not too shiny.) If the dough is not thin enough after you lay it on the cookie sheet, roll it some more, directly on the sheet.

2 Peel and cut the apples in half, core them, and slice each half into ¼-inch slices. Set aside the large center slices of the same size and chop the end slices coarsely. Sprinkle the chopped apple over the dough. Arrange the large slices on the dough beginning at the outside, approximately 1½ inches from the edge. Stagger and overlap the slices to imitate the petals of a flower.

3 Cover the dough completely with a single layer of apples, except for the border. Place smaller slices in the center to resemble the heart of a flower. Bring up the border of the dough and fold it over the apples. Sprinkle the apples with the sugar and pieces of butter, and bake in a 400-degree oven for 65 to 75 minutes, until the galette is really well-browned and crusty.

4 Slide it onto a board. Dilute the apricot preserves with the alcohol (or use 1 tablespoon of water if the jam is thick and you prefer not to use spirits) and spread it on top of the apples with the back of a spoon. Some can also be spread on the top edge of the crust. Follow the design so that you do not disturb the little pieces of apple.

Serve the galette lukewarm, cut into wedges. There are two galettes pictured on the right: in the foreground, a potato galette; in the background, an apple galette.

POTATO GALETTE

A galette isn't necessarily a dessert. The same *pâte brisée* dough covered with tomatoes, sliced onions, olive oil, garlic, and olives is a standard *pissaladière,* a specialty of the south of France. Here is another example, a potato galette, that's wonderfully crusty and thin and quite special. It can be served instead of Yorkshire pudding with a rib roast or a roast leg of lamb, or anywhere a potato dish would go well. It is excellent as a main course on a buffet for a brunch or lunch with a garlicky salad. A successful potato galette has an extra-thin crust and thin slices of potato. Be sure to cook it well.

½ recipe **pâte brisée** *(page 152)*

1 tablespoon butter

1 tablespoon oil

1 pound potatoes, peeled, cut into very thin slices, washed, and dried

½ cup heavy cream

1 Roll out the *pâte brisée* as indicated for the Apple Galette, about ¹⁄₁₆ inch thick and in a 13-inch circle. Place on a large cookie sheet.

2 Melt the butter in a skillet and add the oil. Add the potato slices and sauté for 3 to 4 minutes on high heat until the slices start to look transparent and a few are slightly browned. Let cool a few minutes and spread the potatoes on the dough. Fold over the border of the dough as for Apple Galette.

3 Bake in a 400-degree oven for approximately 45 minutes, until it is nicely browned. Spread the cream on top and bake for another 15 minutes. Serve lukewarm in wedges.

Pâte brisée, a standard pie and pastry dough made with butter, is probably the most useful of all doughs. It can be substituted for puff paste (the multi-layered, very flaky dough used to make Napoleons and puff shells) or sweet pastry dough (the sandy, cookielike dough made of sugar, egg yolk, and flour). It can be used as a pâté dough (a tight, compact dough that can take more abuse, made of egg yolks, lard, and flour). Pate brisée can be used for sweet or savory foods, from pies, and tarts, to quiches and sausages or ham en croûte.

Butter, although a bit more expensive than other shortenings, is much better in pastry for desserts that are to be eaten cold, especially with delicate fruits like raspberries or oranges. Lard or a mixture of lard and butter is satisfactory in a dough used to wrap a sausage or to line a quiche, because the dish is served hot, and the strong flavor of the filling—bacon, mushrooms, cheese, or whatever—makes the delicacy of the pastry less important. In a cold, delicate tart the lard would coat the top of your palate slightly, and its taste would be discernible. Butter, although the most difficult to use, gives the best results.

In a well-made pâte brisée the pieces of butter are visible throughout the dough. If the pieces of butter get completely blended with the flour so that they melt during cooking, the pastry will be tough. The flour and butter must be worked and the water added as fast as possible to obtain a flaky pastry. If you work the dough

3 cups all-purpose flour (dip the measuring cup into the flour, fill it, and level it with your hand)

1 cup (2 sticks) sweet butter, cold, and cut with a knife into thin slices or shavings

½ teaspoon salt

Approximately ¾ cup very cold water

YIELD: ENOUGH PASTRY FOR TWO 13 × 16-INCH RECTANGULAR CRUSTS OR 13-INCH CIRCULAR CRUSTS

⏱ 10 TO 12 MINUTES

too much after adding the water, it will be elastic and chewy. If you use too much butter and not enough water, it will resemble a sweet pastry dough and will be hard to roll thin and pick up from the table; it will be very brittle before and after cooking, sandy, and with no flakiness.

This is a deceptively simple dough. You may get excellent results one time and an ordinary pastry the next. Try it a few times to get a feel for it. Wrapped properly, it can be kept in the refrigerator for 2 or 3 days, or it can be frozen.

1 Mix the flour, butter, and salt together very lightly, so that the pieces of butter remain visible throughout the flour.

2 Add the ice-cold water and mix very fast with your hand just enough that the dough coheres. Cut the dough in half. The pieces of butter should still be visible. Refrigerate for 1 or 2 hours or use it right away. If you use it right away, the butter will be a bit soft, so you may need a little extra flour in the rolling process to absorb it.

3 For one galette, roll half the dough between ⅛ and ¹⁄₁₆ of an inch thick, using flour underneath and on top so that it doesn't stick to the table or the rolling pin. When the dough is the desired shape and thickness, roll it onto the rolling pin and unroll it on the pie plate, tart form, or cookie sheet that you plan to use. Repeat with the other half or reserve for later use. Bake according to the instructions for the particular recipe.

This easy summer dessert takes just a few minutes and is quite delicious. The sliced peaches are arranged in a flower pattern in a gratin or other ovenproof dish, then sweetened with brown sugar, coated with a custard of egg and cream, sprinkled with sliced almonds, and baked in the oven. The same recipe can be made with bananas, plums, pineapple, apple, or just about any soft and juicy fruit—including berries, although they will leak a bit and bleed into the custard. Harder fruits, like pears, unless very ripe, need to be partially precooked before baking.

The same recipe done in a pastry shell becomes a classical fruit quiche. The shell should be precooked for about 20 minutes before the peaches and the custard are added, because the crust takes longer to cook than the custard.

3 ripe peaches (about 1 pound)

⅓ cup brown sugar

1 egg, beaten lightly with a fork

½ cup heavy cream

2 tablespoons sliced almonds

1 tablespoon powdered sugar

S E R V E S   6

🕛 10 TO 15 MINUTES

🕐 35 TO 40 MINUTES

1 Slice the peaches directly on the pit and arrange the segments in a circular pattern in a round, flat, shallow dish like this gratin dish. Complete the circle, then place a few peach slices in the center in a decorative pattern to simulate the center of a flower. Sprinkle the peaches with the brown sugar. Mix the beaten egg with the cream, and pour the mixture on top of the fruit. Sprinkle with the sliced almonds and bake in a 375-degree oven for 35 to 40 minutes.

2 The peaches should be browned and slightly caramelized. Sprinkle with powdered sugar. Let cool to lukewarm before serving.

This is a super-easy dessert to make when you have a few minutes' notice and nothing much at hand. It takes only a few minutes to prepare, a few minutes to cook, and any fruit can be used. It is very good made with pound cake, brioche, or sponge cake, but also quite good on plain slices of white bread. When bread is used, some sugar is added for sweetness, but the sugar is not necessary on sponge or pound cake. The slices of pound cake, about ½ inch thick, should be approximately 4 inches long by 3 inches wide, more or less the size of a slice of bread.

These croûtes are very economical and they can be made with fruits that are a bit past their prime, fruits that have wilted and shriveled. Sour cream is excellent served with these fruit toasts, which can also be served for breakfast or brunch.

2 ounces (½ stick) sweet butter, softened

8 slices bread or cake

Approximately ⅓ to ½ cup sugar

2 ripe medium-size peaches

2 large plums

1 banana

S E R V E S   6   T O   8

🕐 10 MINUTES

🕐 10 MINUTES

1 Spread approximately ½ teaspoon of butter on one side of each slice of bread or cake. Sprinkle ½ teaspoon of sugar on top of the butter on each slice of bread, but not on the cake. Slice the fruits.

2 Arrange the slices of fruit from the outside toward the center to imitate an open flower. Place the sliced banana in the center. It is important to cover all the bread or cake, because the uncovered bread or cake will burn in the oven.

Sprinkle 1 teaspoon of sugar over the fruit on each slice and add 1 teaspoon of butter cut into little dots. Place on a cookie sheet under the broiler, but in the middle of the oven so that it doesn't cook too fast. Broil for 10 minutes. (If your broiler is separate from the oven, bake the croûte at 500 degrees.)

3 Serve right out of the oven; the bread or cake will be moist and sweet underneath, and the fruit barely cooked and a bit caramelized on top. Serve with or without cold sour cream.

ears, available most of the year, are versatile and can be made into several desserts. Bartlett, Comice, and Williams pears cook faster than Seckel or Bosc pears. The cooking time also varies with ripeness. A well-ripened whole pear dropped into hot syrup won't take more than a minute to cook, whereas a hard and unripe pear may take an hour.

White fruits, such as pears, apples, pineapples, or bananas, are often poached in a syrup of water, sugar, lemon juice, and sometimes white wine. Red fruits or berries, such as cherries, plums, or even prunes, tend to be poached in port or red wine. In our recipe, we cook a white fruit with red wine, which tints the flesh a deep mahogany color.

This recipe instructs you to cook the fruit 25 minutes, because that's how long it took the day we made the recipe. You must use your own judgment, however; if the fruit is tender and falling apart after 5 minutes, remove it from the liquid, reduce the syrup by itself, and add it to the fruit. On the other hand, if the fruit is still hard, keep cooking until it is tender when pierced with a fork. When you buy the pears, be sure that they are all equally ripe or unripe so that they require the same cooking time.

4 fairly large Bartlett pears, peeled, quartered, and seeded (1½ pounds)

1½ cups good, strong red wine (Do not use a sweet wine, but rather a Beaujolais, Côte du Rhone, Gamay, or Zinfandel; jug wine will be adequate also)

⅓ cup sugar

Peel of 1 lemon

Juice of 1 lemon (about ⅓ cup)

S E R V E S   6

🕐 10 MINUTES

🕐 30 MINUTES

1 Combine the pears in a pot with the rest of the ingredients. Bring to a boil, cover, and boil the mixture gently about 25 minutes—less if the pears are very ripe, more if they are hard. You should have approximately ⅔ cup of syrup left; if the pears have rendered a lot of liquid, you may have more.

2 Transfer the pears to a bowl. Reduce the syrup to about ⅔ cup, then combine it with the pears. Cool. The liquid should get syrupy.

    Serve in small, deep dishes with some of the syrup and a slice of pound cake or sponge cake. [On the left, Pears in Red Wine; on the right, Pears in Coffee.]

Optional: To fortify the syrup and the taste, add 1 tablespoon of Cognac.

PEARS IN COFFEE

I have had Pears in Coffee many times at the home of a dear friend, Anita Odeurs, who excels at making simple, good home-cooked food.

1 Prepare and serve exactly like Pears in Red Wine. If you want to fortify the syrup, use a tablespoon of Kahlúa.

4 large Bartlett pears, peeled, quartered, and seeded (1½ pounds)

2 cups leftover coffee

⅓ cup brown sugar

1 teaspoon pure vanilla extract

A flambéed dish is always festive. The ingredients are prepared in the kitchen, or right at the table on an alcohol burner or portable gas stove; at the last moment spirits are poured over the dish, a match is touched to it, and *voilà!* Sometimes the flaming is done in the kitchen, but the dish is always presented aflame.

Though flambéing is just a way of making the evaporation of alcohol visible, it is more than a theatrical device. It serves a real purpose in some dishes: It caramelizes sugar in desserts and fruit dishes, and it browns and crisps certain solid foods like crêpes or fish. Sauces are often flambéed, too, though there is nothing to crisp or caramelize; the alcohol is "burned" off, reducing the sharpness and acidity of the spirits (as well as the calories). In a sauce, however, the alcohol would evaporate anyway if brought to a temperature of 160°; the flame is a dramatic touch, but it isn't really necessary.

In order for alcohol to ignite, it has to be hot; if cold, it must be poured onto something hot enough to vaporize it. You must be quick with the match, because the alcohol evaporates within 15 to 20 seconds.

Flambéed Bananas are put together quickly. The lemon, sugar, and butter make a syrup in which the bananas are heated. When everything is hot enough, the rum is added and ignited, and the platter is brought to the table. Rum goes especially well with bananas, but bourbon would be a good choice, too.

4 tablespoons butter

¾ cup brown sugar

6 well-ripened bananas

1 lemon

⅓ cup dark rum

S E R V E S   6

⏲ 5 TO 10 MINUTES

⏱ 10 MINUTES

1 Use a large stainless-steel platter or any platter than can go into the oven. Butter the bottom with half the butter, and sprinkle it with a third of the sugar. Peel the bananas, split them in half and arrange them, flat side down, on the buttered platter.

2 Peel the lemon with a vegetable peeler. Stack the peels into a pile and sliver them into very thin julienne strips. Sprinkle the julienne over the bananas and squeeze the juice from the lemon over all. Add the remaining sugar and butter, and place in a 450-degree oven for 10 minutes.

See to it that everyone is seated at the table before you proceed, then remove the hot platter from the oven. Pour the rum on top (it needn't be heated) and ignite. Using pot holders, bring the platter of flaming bananas into the dining room. Incline the platter slightly so that the juice runs to one side, and spoon the flaming juice back on top of the bananas. Keep basting the bananas with the flaming liquid until the flame dies, then serve.

M E L O N   I N   H O N E Y

You can make this fast dessert with any kind of melon, though a mixture (honeydew and cantaloupe in our recipe) provides attractive contrast in color as well as texture. Choose heavy melons and rely on your nose to find one with a sweet, ripe taste.

4 cups balls, slices, or pieces of a mixture of honeydew and cantaloupe (or other melon)

1 large lime

¼ cup honey

1 tablespoon dark rum (optional)

S E R V E S   6

⏱ 1 0   M I N U T E S

1 Cut the melons in half and remove the seeds. Use a melon baller to make balls, or use a knife to cut the flesh into pieces. Peel the lime with a vegetable peeler. Stack the strips of skin together and mince into a fine julienne. Add them to the melon with the juice of the lime (approximately ⅓ cup) and the honey.

2 Stir the mixture and macerate for 1 hour if time allows. Add a tablespoon of dark rum or another spirit of your choice. Serve in small, deep dishes.

Omelets are more commonly served as a first or main course than as a dessert. However, dessert omelets are classic, particularly those which are stuffed with jam and caramelized with sugar. It is customary to make larger omelets with about 5 eggs to serve 3 to 4 people, rather than individual ones.

The technique for making an omelet is the same whether it is a savory or a dessert. A good pan is imperative. A steel omelet pan is the best because there are no angles, allowing you to make a smooth, round omelet. The pan is indestructible, and for that reason well suited to restaurant use. If it is not used practically every day, however, the eggs will stick. Therefore, a nonstick omelet pan is probably best for home use.

In the French technique, an omelet is made by stirring the eggs with the back of a fork with one hand and agitating the pan with the other, in order to scramble the eggs as fast as possible and to produce the smallest curds so that the omelet is smooth and soft and the mixture well homogenized. The slower the mixing, the larger the curd; the curd size is a matter of personal taste. The eggs are moved constantly so that there is no time for a crust to form on the bottom of the pan, and so that all the eggs cook at once instead of layer by layer. When the mixture is solid, it is brought to one end of the inclined pan so that less of the surface is exposed to the heat, then left for 10 to 15 seconds so that a light skin forms

5 eggs
2 teaspoons sugar
1 tablespoon butter
⅓ cup apricot jam
1 to 2 tablespoons powdered sugar
⅓ cup Cognac or other brandy to flambé (optional)

S E R V E S   3   T O   4

⊎ ⏲ 1 5   M I N U T E S

on the bottom to enclose the omelet. The two "lips" of the omelet are brought together, the stuffing is added in the center, and the omelet is finally inverted on a plate. In our case, the stuffing is apricot jam. They can also be stuffed with fresh fruit and served with a sauce, or even flambéed.

1 Beat the eggs and sugar with a fork so that the mixture is well combined and no little pieces of white are showing.
Melt the butter in an 8-inch nonstick skillet or omelet pan, and when it starts to foam but is not too hot, add the eggs. (The eggs will set too fast, form a skin, and wrinkle if the butter is too hot and smoky.) With one hand stir the eggs with a fork, and shake the pan with the other hand. It should take approximately 1 minute on medium heat for the eggs to set.

2 Incline the pan so that the eggs gather at one side when you stir for the last time. Hit the pan lightly on the corner of the stove to make sure that the eggs lie flat underneath, and let them cook for 10 to 15 seconds to form a thin skin. Bring one lip toward the center, folding it and pressing it into place with the back of the fork.

3 Hold the pan in one hand, and with the other bang lightly at the junction of the handle to flip the omelet slightly into the skillet and to make the second lip come up so that it can be folded to meet the first lip. Spoon the jam between the lips. Hold the pan with one hand, hold a platter close to the pan with other, and invert the omelet onto the platter. If the omelet is not shaped right, press it into a nice oval with a kitchen towel.

4 Sprinkle the omelet with powdered sugar. Heat a metal skewer in the flame of the stove until it is red, and mark a latticework with it on top of the omelet. The omelet is served this way or flambéed.

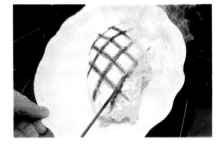

To flambé the omelet (see also page 159), heat the alcohol gently until lukewarm to hot; do not let it boil. Pour the hot alcohol on top of the omelet and ignite it right away. Tip the platter and spoon the liquid back onto the omelet. Keep basting until it stops flaming. Serve at once.

A crêpe is an unleavened, flat, thin pancake of cooked dough or batter which is used as a wrapper for another food. Crêpes can be served as a dessert; stuffed with ham, fish, spinach or the like as a main course; or stuffed with cheese and cut into tidbits as a hot hors d'oeuvre. Some type of crêpe is made in most cuisines the world over. There is the Italian crespella, the French crêpe, the Chinese mandarin pancake, the Mexican tortilla, and the Russian blinchki. In France the crêpe used to be called *pannequet,* from which the word *pancake* is probably derived. A very thin *pannequet* resembles the wrinkled, fragile-looking fabric which we know as crêpe—hence its name. It is sometimes called *crêpe dentelle* because of the tiny lacy holes at the edges.

The quantity of liquid in the batter can be changed to make the crêpe thicker or thinner. Milk or a mixture of milk and water is usually used, but some recipes use cream or even beer. Cream or extra egg yolks make a crêpe that is tender, soft, and difficult to turn. The more water and the less fat, the more it is like bread dough, making a crêpe that's tougher and more elastic. The number of eggs varies from recipe to recipe as well.

The batter does not have to rest and set before it can be used. If it sets, it gets more elastic and stronger, but in the final product this is hardly noticeable.

There are special steel crêpe pans, 4 to 5 inches in diameter, that have very short sides,

1 ½ cups all-purpose flour (dip the measuring cup directly into the flour bin and level it off with your hand)

3 eggs

1 cup milk

⅓ stick butter, melted

½ teaspoon salt

½ teaspoon sugar

1 cup cold water

1 tablespoon oil

YIELD: 2 DOZEN CRÊPES

⏱ 5 TO 10 MINUTES

🍳 20 TO 30 MINUTES

which makes the crêpe easy to flip. Any pan that has a nonstick surface works just as well, and does not have to be seasoned. We use a pan 7 to 8 inches in diameter. It makes a larger crêpe, and the whole process goes faster.

As you make the crêpes, stack them one on top of the other to prevent them from drying out. Crêpes can be made ahead of time and reheated, especially when they are to be stuffed or used in Crêpes Suzette. If you cover them with plastic wrap so that they do not dehydrate and absorb other flavors, they will last a few days in the refrigerator. They can also be frozen.

To me, the best way to eat crêpes is the way we did it at home as children. We picked them piping hot out of the skillet and ate them plain, with sugar sprinkled on top, or with jam, or sometimes with butter and sugar, or grated chocolate. With burned fingers and mouth, we had the best time ever, and crêpes have never tasted as good since.

1 In a bowl combine the flour, eggs, ½ cup milk, melted butter, salt, and sugar. Mix well with a whisk. The batter should be very thick; it is easier to get rid of lumps in a thick batter than in a thin one. Work it until it is smooth, then add the other ½ cup of milk, the cold water, and the oil. Stir well.

Heat the skillet and butter it lightly for the first crêpe. I am always telling my students in cooking class that "The pan has to get in the mood." Pour about 2 tablespoonfuls of batter on one side of the skillet. Immediately tip the skillet, shaking it at the same time to make the batter run all over the bottom. The speed at which the batter is spread determines the thickness of the crêpe. If you do not move the skillet fast enough, the batter sets before it has a chance to spread and the crêpe will be thick.

2 Cook it on medium to high heat for about 30 seconds. To flip, bang the skillet on a pot holder on the corner of the stove to get the crêpe loose, and flip it over.

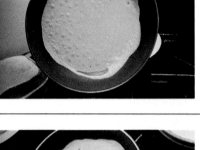

3 An alternate way to flip the crêpe is to lift it with a spatula and with the other hand to grab the edge of the crêpe. Then rest the spatula on the side of the skillet and turn the crêpe over with both hands.

4 Cook it about 20 to 25 seconds on the other side, and transfer it to a plate. Repeat with the remaining batter. Notice that the side of the crêpe that browned first has the nicer color. Be sure to serve the crêpe so that this is the side that is visible.

Serve the crêpes with an array of jams, such as strawberry, raspberry, or apricot preserves, or with apple butter or honey, or with sugar and butter or grated chocolate.

In restaurants Crêpes Suzette are made right at the table. Lumps of sugar are rubbed over oranges to absorb the essential oil in the skins, then cooked with butter and orange juice almost to a caramel. The crêpes are dipped in the mixture to coat them on each side, then sprinkled with Cognac and Grand Marnier and flamed. Made this way, however, only 3 or 4 crêpes can be flambéed at a time, so it is a less than ideal method for serving a whole family at home. We use an alternate method.

The orange butter is excellent by itself spread on cake layers as an orange buttercream.

1 dozen crêpes (page 166)

SUZETTE BUTTER

¾ stick butter

¼ cup sugar

Peel of 1 orange removed with a vegetable peeler

Juice of 1 orange (⅓ to ½ cup)

2 tablespoons sugar

TO FLAME

½ cup Cognac or brandy

¼ cup Grand Marnier or homemade orange liqueur

S E R V E S   6

🕐 10 TO 15 MINUTES

🕐 5   MINUTES

1 Place the butter, sugar, and orange peel in the bowl of a food processor and process until the orange peels are no longer visible and the whole mixture is a uniform orange color. Add the juice slowly with the machine on so that the butter absorbs it.

2 Spread approximately 1 tablespoon of the orange butter on each crêpe, and fold the crêpes in fourths. Butter generously a large ovenproof platter (ours is 17 inches long by 10 inches wide) and sprinkle it with sugar. Arrange one dozen stuffed crêpes on it, overlapping slightly, but leave a space at the end of the platter where the sauce can accumulate.

3 Sprinkle the crêpes with 2 tablespoons of sugar and place them under the broiler, approximately in the middle of the oven if your broiler is in the same unit, for about 2 to 3 minutes. The surface of the crêpes will caramelize.

   Pour ½ cup of Cognac or brandy and ¼ cup Grand Marnier or homemade orange liqueur on the very hot crêpes and ignite. (See also page 182 on flambéing.) Bring the platter to the table and incline it slightly so that the flaming juices gather in the space you left. Spoon up the liquid and pour it back, still flaming, onto the crêpes. When the flame subsides, serve two crêpes per person with some of the sauce.

HOMEMADE ORANGE LIQUEUR: Grand Marnier, a liqueur made of Cognac and a distillate of oranges, is very expensive, and so we offer you an alternative: homemade orange liqueur.

1 Peel 7 to 8 oranges with a vegetable peeler. Place the skin in a bottle and cover it with 3 cups of brandy. Add 2 tablespoons sugar. Shake the bottle a few times to dissolve the sugar. Then let it stand for approximately 3 weeks to 1 month and you will have a very good orange brandy.

These crêpes are folded over to enclose a soufflé mixture, then baked in the oven where they puff like a soufflé, becoming very light and pretty.

Any soufflé mixture can be used, though we use a cross between an orange soufflé base and a meringue mixture. The egg whites, and the fact that there's no flour in the soufflé base, make it extremely light.

1 tablespoon butter

2 tablespoons plus ⅔ cup sugar

Peel of 1 large orange (removed with vegetable peeler)

5 egg whites

9 crêpes (page 166)

Powdered sugar for dusting

S E R V E S 6

⏲ 1 5 M I N U T E S

⏱ 1 2 M I N U T E S

1 Butter a large stainless-steel or other ovenproof platter and sprinkle it with 2 tablespoons sugar.

Place the remaining sugar together with the orange peel in a food processor and process until the peel has been completely chopped and absorbed into the sugar.

Beat the egg whites until firm (see page 49 for explanation of beating egg whites) and add the sugar mixture fairly quickly. Beat for another 30 seconds until the mixture is fluffy and shiny.

Arrange 6 crêpes on the platter so that half of each one hangs over the edge. Place ½ to ¾ cup of the beaten egg whites on each crêpe and fold the other half over. Place 2 or 3 more stuffed crêpes in the center of the tray.

2 Sprinkle the crêpes with 1 tablespoon of powdered sugar and place in a 350-degree oven for about 12 minutes. Sprinkle with a bit more powdered sugar and serve right away.

These puffs made of *pâte à choux* are ideal as a winter dessert. They are extremely light and delicious, in addition to being inexpensive and easy to make. The dough can be flavored with vanilla, lemon, almond extract, coffee, or even chocolate. Our dough contains vanilla and sugar, but in France it is often made with orange-blossom water, which has a very distinctive taste. The dough can be made a week or more ahead and kept in the refrigerator, and the puffs can be made quickly at the last moment.

The secret of these puffs is the size and the time of cooking. The balls should not be too big—about 1 ½ teaspoons of dough—and they should be cooked long enough for the mixture to be completely done and expand without a crust forming too fast.

1 cup milk
1 ⅓ ounces (⅓ stick) sweet butter
2 teaspoons sugar
1 teaspoon vanilla
1 cup flour (dip the measuring cup into the bin and level it off)
3 eggs
4 to 5 cups oil
Powdered sugar to sprinkle on top

S E R V E S   6   T O   8;
A P P R O X I M A T E L Y
3   D O Z E N   P U F F S

🕐 10 MINUTES
🕐 15 MINUTES

1 Combine the milk, butter, sugar, and vanilla in a saucepan and bring to a boil. As soon as the mixture boils, add the flour all at once and combine well and fast with a wooden spatula. Stir the mixture until it forms a ball and separates from the sides of the pan; this will take only a few seconds (see the Parisienne Gnocchi, page 38). Keep cooking and stirring the mixture for 30 seconds to a minute to dry it further.

2 Transfer the dough to a clean bowl or to the bowl of an electric mixer. Let cool for 5 minutes and add 1 egg. Stir the mixture until the egg is incorporated. The dough will first be very loose and in pieces. Keep stirring; it will eventually cohere. Add the second egg in the same manner, and finally the third.

Cover the dough with an oiled piece of plastic wrap, and refrigerate until ready to use. It should be cool when used.

Heat the oil to 325 to 350 degrees. Scoop up about 1 ½ teaspoons of dough and, with your index finger, push the mixture to the edge of the spoon. Let it drop into the hot oil, but work close to the oil to prevent splashing.

3 Let the fritters cook for 7 to 8 minutes at the same temperature. The balls will float to the top and turn around by themselves as they brown and expand. They should be almost hollow inside, very light and very delicate. Remove the puffs from the oil and drain them on paper towels.

4 Arrange the fritters on a serving dish. Sprinkle generously with powdered sugar, and serve as soon as possible. (See note on page 179 about reusing oil for deep-frying.)

This type of cream or mousse is both beautiful and easy to make. It can also be used between cake layers instead of buttercream, or to stuff profiteroles, puffs, éclairs, or other pastries. The coffee blends beautifully with the chocolate. Our recipe is not too sweet, though it could be made sweeter to please different tastes. You can make it a day or two ahead, but cover it tightly with plastic wrap and refrigerate it. Cream desserts, especially chocolate, will absorb tastes in the refrigerator, from celery to onions to meat or fish. Mold in individual dishes or a large bowl.

3 tablespoons dry instant coffee

1 envelope plain gelatin

¼ cup boiling water

2 cups heavy cream

2 tablespoons sugar

½ ounce unsweetened chocolate

1 ounce semisweet chocolate

S E R V E S   6   T O   8

⏱ 10 T O 15 M I N U T E S

1 Combine the 3 tablespoons of dry coffee with the gelatin in a saucepan and add the boiling water. Stir the mixture gently on low heat until the coffee and gelatin are completely dissolved.

Place the heavy cream and sugar in a bowl and beat by hand or by machine until the mixture is fluffy and holds a stiff peak, but is not grainy. Be careful not to overbeat or the cream will turn into butter.

2 Pour the coffee-gelatin mixture into the whipped cream all at once, and beat rapidly with a whisk for 20 to 30 seconds, until the mixture sets. In the photograph the cream is already quite hard, but it will get even harder after 1 hour in the refrigerator.

3 Melt the unsweetened and semisweet chocolates together. Place the coffee cream in individual dishes or in a large bowl and drizzle the chocolate over the top in a design. Refrigerate at least half an hour before serving. It is excellent served with slices of brioche, pound cake, or sponge cake. If the cake is a bit stale, toast it before serving with the cream.

In the last few pages of this book I've taken the opportunity to high-light some of the information contained in the body of the recipes and address in more depth some of the questions about basic cooking techniques brought up by viewers and readers. All these points have broad application. For instance, if you learn how to avoid lumps in your apple fritter batter, then all your other batters will be smooth, too. Like-wise, if you understand how preparation affects the potency of garlic, you'll know how to achieve the result you want. If you learn how to properly prepare a hard-cooked egg for the Eggs Jeannette, you'll never suffer from green yolks and rubbery whites again. Mastery of these simple fundamental principles makes it all so much easier. So enjoy—happy cooking!

B E U R R E   M A N I É

When making a *beurre manié,* be sure the butter has softened to room tempera-ture. Put the butter and the flour in a small bowl and whisk them together. This is the best way to make a *beurre manié,* even if you are working with very small quantities of flour and butter. Not only does the whisk combine the flour and butter, but the resulting paste attaches to the threads of the whisk, so that you can plunge it directly into the boiling liquid and begin whisking to incorporate it into the sauce.

B R E A D

To freshen stale bread: French bread is best within hours of being baked. Within one day—especially with commercially made bread—it loses its moisture and dries out, particularly the long, narrow, tapered baguette. If kept in a plastic bag, it remains moist but gets soggy and soft.

To freshen a French baguette, pass it briefly under running water, lightly wetting it all around, then place in a 400-degree oven for 10 to 12 minutes. It will crisp again, becoming flavorful and crunchy. Serve as soon as possible, as it will dry out this time and crumble even faster than it did the first.

Stale bread can always be used for bread crumbs or in dishes such as the Stuffed Lamb Breast (page 113) or the Bread Galette (page 32) as well as the

Apple Brown Betty (page 148). It can also be used for croûtons if it can be cut without crumbling.

Croûtes, croûtons, and toasts: These terms are often used interchangeably, which is understandable as there's a fuzzy line between them, though distinctions in shape and use can be made.

A croûte (as in the Croûte of Fruit on page 155) is usually a receptacle for a savory or sweet filling or topping. It can be a thick slice of bread or cake or a roll or brioche hollowed out to accommodate a filling.

Croûtons, on the other hand, are generally used as a garnish. They can be cut into little cubes like those used to garnish the Sautéed Whiting or into larger slices like those used in the Fish Soup.

Small croûtons are best sautéed in a mixture of butter and oil (see page 79), whereas the larger slices of bread can be pressed lightly on both sides onto an oil-coated cookie sheet, then browned on the same sheet in the oven. This particular technique for oiling and browning (see page 26 for more details) gives excellent results and uses a minimum of oil.

There is no comparison between homemade croûtons and store-bought croûtons, which usually taste stale and rancid.

When bread is sliced and toasted—that is to say, browned without fat—it's usually called a toast, like our Melba Toast on page 55. Toasts are basically used for sandwiches.

C E L E R Y

Stringiness: The inner stalks of celery are more tender than the large, dark outside ones. When used for flavoring, as in a stock, the tougher outer stalks are fine to use as is, but when served as a garnish, they should be peeled with a vegetable peeler to remove the uppermost coarse layers of fibers. The peelings can then be used in stocks.

C H I C K E N

To bone: Boning chicken always seems difficult to many cooks, yet it is fairly simple if one remembers a few simple rules. The most common mistake people make is to use a knife far too much in the boning process. Basically, the breast is held to the carcass by the shoulder joints, and the two legs are held by the hip joints which are next to the small oysters on the side of the back. These are the only places which must be cut through with a knife; all the rest of the boning is done mostly by just pulling the meat from the bone. Therefore, rather than cutting there is much more pulling and tearing, which is not only faster but gives better results. Step-by-step instructions can be found on page 99.

C O R N

To remove kernels: There are different techniques for removing corn kernels from the cob. The more conventional way is to stand the ear on end and slice the kernels off with a sharp knife. However, it is probably safer to lay the cob on its side and slice off the kernels in strips. For more information, refer to the photograph that accompanies the recipe for Corn Chowder on page 29.

D E E P   F R Y I N G

Reusing oil: Deep frying is primarily a restaurant operation because in a restaurant the oil is used, strained, and replenished daily and therefore doesn't get rancid or wasted. At home, what to do with the oil once it's been used is often a problem. My feeling is that it should be strained through layers of paper towels and reused as soon as possible, as it doesn't keep indefinitely.

Once you've used oil for frying fish, or anything else strong-tasting, you shouldn't reuse it for something more delicate. The ideal order of use would be to go from the most delicate to the strongest: from simple, clean, sliced vegetables or fruits to breaded or batter-fried vegetables, to poultry, to meat, then finally fish. If the oil has been overused it will smell, form a very thick foam when heated, and no longer brown food well.

Deep frying means frying in enough fat to thoroughly cover the food. Use an oil that is tasteless so it doesn't obscure the taste of the food. Most vegetable oils on the market fall into this category. Certain oils such as cottonseed oil or grapeseed oil can withstand higher temperatures and are ideal for frying.

D O U G H

Lard or butter in dough: Dough made with butter is usually the hardest to make well, though if handled properly it gives the best taste by far. There is more moisture in butter than in other types of fat, which gives elasticity to the dough and makes it trickier to work with.

In some recipes it is imperative to use butter, while at other times a mixture of butter and lard gives an equally good result. A precooked pie crust filled with a lemon cream or fresh raspberries would require butter because the filling is delicate and the pie is served cold, which makes the taste of the fat most detectable. On the other hand, a dough used to encase a pâté mixture or sausage, or used for a quiche, can be made with lard or a mixture of lard and butter. Some of the fat from the pâté or sausage will be absorbed by the dough anyway. More importantly, the dough will be served hot or warm, and the strong flavoring of the ingredients in a quiche—whether bacon, ham, mushrooms, or herbs—will overpower the taste of the fat.

E G G S

To hard-cook: It is astonishing that such a simple thing as a hard-cooked egg can be as consistently bad as it is in most coffee shops and restaurants. The problem is either cooking too long, cooking at too strong a boil, or not allowing the eggs to cool completely in cold water after cooking.

To hard-cook eggs, cover them completely with tap or boiling water. Bring the water to a simmer and simmer gently for approximately 9 or 10 minutes. One or two minutes more will not affect them much, provided the eggs aren't allowed to boil strongly, which toughens the whites, making them rubbery and hard. More importantly, the eggs should be placed under cold running water until they are *completely* cool. If not, the surface of the yolk will turn green and acquire a slightly acrid taste.

To beat egg whites: The temperature of egg whites affects how they beat. The bubbles forced into the whites during beating are larger if the eggs are at room temperature and smaller if they are cold. The larger the bubbles the greater the volume of beaten whites.

Generally, as volume is desirable, it would make sense to use room-temperature eggs. However, this is only so if you have good-quality, farm-fresh eggs. Supermarket eggs, which are neither high in quality nor too fresh, should be used straight from the refrigerator, as when beaten at room temperature they tend to overheat, become weepy and grainy, and cause problems.

F I S H

Buying fish: When buying fresh fish, check to be sure the scales are shiny and firmly attached to the body, the eyes clear, the gills pink, and the flesh firm. It is easier to recognize freshness in a whole fish than in fillets, so try to buy whole fish. Above all, rely on your nose—very fresh fish has no smell at all.

Very often the so-called fresh fish—usually defined as fish that has never been frozen—may have been sitting on ice for days. In that case you're probably better off with fish that's been frozen fresh and properly defrosted.

When buying frozen fish it's a question of common sense. Be aware that the whole fish or larger fillets will suffer less from freezing than thin fillets which dehydrate and often get freezer burn. Defrost the fish slowly, still wrapped, under refrigeration.

About fish stocks: Fish heads and bones give fish stocks, soups, and chowders their distinct flavors. The best bones and heads to use are from flat fish, such as sole, dab, flounder, or halibut. Collarbones from cod are also good. Oily fish such as mackerel, bluefish, salmon, herring, and tuna are less desirable.

When bones and heads for fish stock are not available, buy whole fish, gut and fillet them, and use the bones and heads for the stock, reserving the fillets for an entrée. Alternately, when you're cooking fillets, buy a whole fish and freeze the bones and heads for later use. For a recipe for a good fish chowder made from bones and heads, turn to page 24. For a recipe using fish fillets, see page 82.

Sautéing fish: The common pitfalls when sautéing fish are that the fish may fall apart, or stick to the pan, or not develop a crusty outside. To remedy, first of all use a heavy aluminum, cast-iron, or copper skillet. Second, be sure that the fish is dry before dredging with flour. If it is not dry, the moisture will turn the flour into a paste. (A coating of flour gives the outside of the fish a good crust.) Do not flour the fish too far in advance as the flour will become soggy. Third, be sure the mixture of oil and butter is hot before adding your fish and, especially, do not crowd the skillet. Sauté the fish on a brisk medium to high flame, especially during the first five minutes of cooking, to create a crust.

If the fish is large you'll need to cover it to finish cooking. Be sure to brown on each side uncovered first, then cover it during the last period of cooking.

Fish roe: Overlooked, though excellent and inexpensive, is ordinary fish roe (not just shad or sturgeon). Fish liver is also quite good, as is the milt. For more information about these less commonly used parts of the fish, see the recipe for sautéed whiting roe and liver on page 80.

F L A M B É I N G

Igniting vapor: When alcohol is heated to a certain temperature it rises as vapor and evaporates. If you are ready with a match you can ignite the vapor and see it in the form of flames. Flambéing makes the evaporation of alcohol visible. It also lends a dramatic touch to the presentation of a dish. In the case of Crêpes Suzette, it caramelizes the sugar and browns the dish. In other cases, such as with fish and lobster, it sears the meat and gives it added taste and texture.

To flambé, either the food must be very hot or the alcohol lukewarm in order for it to ignite. Be sure to be quick with the match, as the alcohol evaporates within 15 to 20 seconds, after which there will be no vapor left to flame.

F L O U R   L U M P I N G

To avoid lumping in batters: In all mixtures made with flour and liquid, which includes batters for fritters, crêpes, cakes, and the like, the mixture may get lumpy if the liquid and the flour are not combined properly. When too much liquid is added at the beginning, even when a whisk is used, the flour will form lumps. Because of the thinness of the batter these lumps won't encounter any resistance when worked with the whisk. They will just move about in the batter without smoothing out. To avoid lumping, add half to two-thirds of the liquid to the mixture so that it's thick and the threads of the whisk meet enough resistance to work any lumps into a smooth, shiny mass. At that point, there's no danger in adding the rest of the liquid as there is no dry flour left. The liquid will combine easily with the thick batter.

F R U I T

To poach: Cooking time and seasoning for fruit vary according to the ripeness of the fruit. A hard, unripe pear, for example, may have to be poached in a syrup for an hour to be tender and more sugar and lemon used to compensate for the blandness of unripe fruit. On the other hand, a very ripe pear will poach in one or two minutes. Test for doneness by piercing the fruit with a fork; it should be tender but not so soft that it falls apart. It is important to use fruits that are all equally ripe or unripe so that they require the same cooking time. Turn to page 135 for a recipe for poached oranges and to page 157 for poached pears.

Candied citrus peels: Candying your own peels is truly rewarding as you create, for practically no money at all, a product that's far superior to anything available in the supermarkets, while using a part of the fruit that would otherwise be discarded. You can buy quality candied peels at specialty stores, but they cost a small fortune—whereas your own are effectively for free. Candied peels are extremely versatile; an assortment of things you can do with them is detailed on pages 131–134.

G A R L I C

Potency: When garlic is finely chopped and used raw, as in *aïoli* or *rouille* or any other of the sauces from the south of France, its flavor is the most pronounced. If cooked just briefly, as in French escargots or Italian scampi, or when mixed with parsley and sprinkled on top of sautéed potatoes or zucchini, the garlic still remains quite strong.

Yet several heads of garlic—as many as 50 or 60 cloves—separated and cooked in their skin along with a roast will come out of the oven so mild you can serve them along with the roast. The flesh can either be sucked from the clove or pressed out with a fork, then spread on bread and dipped in the juices from the roast. Delicious!

How you use garlic in a dish—the form in which you add the garlic as well as the amount—depends on the result you are looking for. All you need to remember is that raw garlic, finely chopped or puréed, is at the top of the scale in potency, whereas slowly cooked, unpeeled cloves are at the bottom. Peeled and cracked whole cloves and sliced cloves fall in between, and both are stronger raw than cooked.

To peel, crush, and chop garlic: Separate the cloves from the garlic head by placing the head of garlic on its side and hitting it with the palm of your hand. Using the flat side of a heavy knife, smack the clove just enough to crack the shell open. Remove the clove from the shell and cut off the root end and any damaged parts. Place the blade flat on the clove and smack it down and forward to crush the clove to a pulp. Crushing releases the essential oils and simultaneously makes the garlic easier to chop. Chop to a purée.

G R A T I N S

Gratin or *gratiné* means "crusted" in French and a gratin can be any dish that comes out of the oven with a crust on top. For a gratin, the food is usually spread out in a fairly shallow baking dish and topped with cheese, bread crumbs, eggs, or a white sauce to form a crust. Gratins generally cook quickly (see for example the Peach Gratiné on page 154, or the Gratin of Cabbage on page 59, or the one of eggs on page 37). They are also good vehicles for leftovers. See the Gratin of Pasta with Vegetables on page 41, for example, or the Gratin Parmentier, page 123.

L I V E R

Proportions and procedures when using liver in a pâté: When a pâté mixture is made with liver, regardless of whether it is pork, chicken, or calf's liver, it is important to respect certain proportions and certain procedures. A common pitfall is to add too much liver, which makes the pâté dark, bitter, and too strong. Another pitfall is to cook pâté too fast, which renders the fat from the meat, making the pâté grainy and dry.

If the liver is only coarsely chopped, dry and strong-tasting dark pieces will be apparent throughout the cooked pâté and it won't bind the pâté as it should. Puréed liver acts as a binding agent, holding everything together and preventing the fat from running out while cooking. The liver can be puréed by itself or with the fat, at which point it practically liquefies.

The Chicken Liver Pâté on page 51 is really more of a mousse than a pâté. It is made with precooked livers and then refrigerated, unlike country pâté, which is made with meats, liver, and fat and baked for a long time in the oven.

M U S S E L S

To clean: Buy medium-sized mussels, about 15 to 18 per pound, as the larger mussels tend to be tough. Check to see if an open mussel is alive by placing it in cold water or tickling the inside with the point of a knife. If it closes, it is alive and well.

Mussels must be washed and cleaned carefully. Leave them in one or two gallons of cold water with a handful of salt for an hour or so. They will disgorge some of the sand. Clean the mussels by rubbing them against each other vigorously. To check tightly closed mussels for mud, try to slide the shells apart in opposite directions with your fingers. If the mussel is full of mud, discard it.

Once cleaned and separated, mussels can be kept in the refrigerator for 3 or 4 days before cooking.

O N I O N S

To wash: To prevent chopped onions from discoloring when served raw, as for steak tartare or gazpacho, or with caviar, carpaccio, and the like, place them in a strainer and toss them briefly under cold running water. When well rinsed, press them by hand or in a cloth towel to extrude the water. The onions will be white and fluffy. They will keep several days without darkening. This procedure can also be used when onions are too strong: It removes some of their sharpness.

P E P P E R S

To skin: Although it's not necessary to remove the skin from peppers, it does improve the texture and the taste in certain recipes, such as the one for marinated peppers on page 68. To skin, you have to char or cook the peppers until they are blistered all around. Then enclose them in a plastic bag so they steam in their own heat for ten minutes. The skin will then slide off easily.

S A L T I N G

Salting vegetables: Salt draws moisture out of vegetables, just as it does with meats. Salting cucumbers makes them look limp but, paradoxically, it keeps them crunchy for days. (The same technique is used for pickles.)

We salt tomatoes when we're making a dressed tomato salad that won't be served right away. By salting and draining them before dressing, the salad doesn't become liquidy. When tomatoes are too watery, which they tend to be at certain times of the year, salting and draining them makes them more flavorful. When they're less watery, the taste is denser.

Salting eggplant not only draws out the moisture, removing with it some of the eggplant's bitterness, but it makes it less porous. This makes the eggplant absorb less oil during frying. More about eggplant is covered in the recipe on page 57.

Other vegetables with a high moisture content, such as zucchini or other squash, can be handled in the same way.

S A U C E S

Boiling starch-based sauces: Often cooks are puzzled by a flour- or other starch-based sauce which suddenly thins down during cooking for no apparent reason. Certain cookbooks advise not to boil delicate starches like arrowroot, chestnut powder, or even cornstarch to prevent thinning. From my experience you can boil any type of starch from a regular *roux* made with flour to arrowroot, cornstarch, potato starch, or rice flour, and it will sometimes thin down and sometimes won't.

Years ago in the Plaza Athenée in Paris I recall making "the mother sauces," or *les grandes sauces* (béchamel and velouté), with a variety of starches. These sauces were cooked for at least two hours on top of the stove. By then the thick, heavy sauce had stabilized, and had there been any danger of it thinning out it would have already happened.

Those thick sauces were used in turn as thickening agents for derivative sauces *(les petites sauces).* For example, in a fish sauce the fish broth and cream were thickened with a tablespoon of fish velouté. When doing a soufflé we'd use a precooked béchamel, adding the egg yolks and beaten whites, knowing that the béchamel had cooked long enough to stabilize. There was no danger that the mixture would thin down in the oven and split.

This system, of course, is restaurant practice and has no place at home, but it's good to know that sudden thinning of sauces happens to professionals as well and, also, what the chef does to remedy the problem.

Back to the home kitchen: In my experience a sauce may or may not thin, regardless of the type of starch used and regardless of the cooking temperature. It seems that the coagulating element in the sauce breaks down for some reason at some point but, besides all the advice given in books, in practice I have never found a pattern or reason why a starch may or may not break down.

The mixture of a cold liquid and starch—such as arrowroot or cornstarch—when added to a liquid that is at least 180 degrees will thicken the hot liquid as it is stirred in. These fast-thickening starches are ideal for correcting the breakdown of a sauce because you can add a little at a time and monitor the results. The starch should always be diluted with a cold liquid.

S K I L L E T S

For omelets and crêpes: In a professional kitchen, steel pans are used for omelets as well as for crêpes. The heat transfer in these pans is very fast, they are practically indestructible, and the omelets and crêpes made in them never stick for the simple reason that they are in constant use. At home, the same pan has to be reseasoned practically every time you use it.

For this reason, a nonstick pan is the best type of pan for making crêpes and omelets at home. It doesn't discolor, it won't stick, and it is easy to work with. In a restaurant, that same nonstick pan—with the rough treatment of restaurant use and a dishwasher—would probably be destroyed in a matter of days.

S O U P S

To thicken: Soup can be made with water and a few pieces of vegetables, but to give it body you may want to thicken it during the cooking process or at the end with one or another of the following thickening agents.

Leftover bread—toasted or untoasted—can be placed in the bottom of each soup bowl and the soup poured on top. To thicken soup while it is still cooking, whisk in a *roux* (a mixture of butter and flour) and keep cooking for at least 10 minutes before serving. Other thickening agents include potato or rice flour, as well as cornstarch, which should be diluted with a cold liquid before being stirred into the soup. Of course any type of pasta, from pastina to noodles, as well as rice, tapioca, semolina, farina, couscous, and oatmeal flakes can be sprinkled on top of the soup, stirred in and cooked just long enough to thicken.

T O M A T O E S

To skin: It is not absolutely necessary to skin and peel tomatoes. However, it often makes a sauce or a salad a bit more elegant. The skin as well as the seeds and juice can be used in a stock or brown sauce.

There are different methods of removing skin—all viable. If you need to peel just one tomato, you might cut off the peel with a knife. Or you might impale the tomato on a fork and roast it for 10 to 30 seconds, depending on the ripeness of the tomato, over a gas flame. Then peel the skin off with a knife.

One of the most common methods, particularly efficient when peeling a lot of tomatoes, is to lower them into boiling liquid. Immerse very ripe tomatoes for only 10 seconds; hothouse winter tomatoes may take up to 45 seconds. Run under cold water and peel the skins off when cool.

A C K N O W L E D G M E N T S

The making of a book is a complex endeavor, and it is never completely possible to thank all the persons responsible for its coming out. A few, however, are so tightly linked with the book that they share its fatherhood directly with the author. Among those, I first want to thank my dear editor and friend, Ann Bramson, whose quest for quality is reflected on each page of this book; Leon Perer, my indefatigable photographer; Gloria, my supportive wife; Cynthia Warshaw, who struggled with the manuscript, smiling; Grandpa and Ethel; as well as the tasters Gloria, Ben, Beverly and Marvin Zimmerman, and Pat and Bernie LaRivière. Finally, a special "thank you" to my mother, aunts, and cousins, who have inspired me and instilled in me throughout my youth that love for true, honest, and simple home cooking.